Body Self
&
Psychological Self

A DEVELOPMENTAL AND CLINICAL INTEGRATION OF DISORDERS OF THE SELF

By

David W. Krueger, M.D.

BRUNNER/MAZEL *Publishers* • New York

Excerpt from "Little Gidding" in *Four Quartets,* copyright 1943 by T. S. Eliot, renewed 1971 by Esme Valerie Eliot. Reprinted by permission of Harcourt Brace Jovanovich, Inc.

Library of Congress Cataloging-in-Publication Data

Krueger, David W.
    Body self & psychological self : a developmental and clinical integration of disorders of the self / by David W. Krueger.
        p. cm.
    Includes bibliographies and index.
    ISBN 0-87630-543-5
    1. Self. 2. Body image. 3. Personality disorders. 4. Medicine, Psychosomatic. I. Title. II. Title: Body self and psychological self.
        [DNLM: 1. Body Image. 2. Personality Disorders.
    3. Psychoanalytic Therapy. 4. Psychophysiologic Disorders. 5. Self Concept. BF 697 K94b]
    RC455.4.S42K78 1989
    616.85'8—dc 19
    DNLM/DLC
    for Library of Congress   88-26256
                                                                    CIP

Copyright © 1989 by David W. Krueger, M.D.

Published by
BRUNNER/MAZEL, INC.
19 Union Square
New York, New York 10003

MANUFACTURED IN THE UNITED STATES OF AMERICA

10 9 8 7 6 5 4 3 2 1

We shall not cease from exploration
And the end of all our exploring
Will be to arrive where we started
And know the place for the first time.
                                        —T. S. Eliot
        "Little Gidding" from *Four Quartets*

Contents

Introduction

Although Freud recognized the body ego as the foundation for subsequent ego development, the body and its evolving mental representation have been largely omitted from developmental and psychoanalytic theory. The absence of a developmental model of the body self—its formation, maturational evolution, the integration of body and psyche, and related psychopathologies—has led clinicians in psychotherapy and psychoanalysis to focus nearly exclusively on the psychological self without sufficient regard for the body self as container and foundation of the psychological self. Our patients speak most vividly; their lexicon is emotional, behavioral, and psychosomatic symptomatology, while their bodies are often their language.

The collaborative work resulting in this book began with treatment of eating-disordered patients, now numbering over four hundred in both inpatient and outpatient settings. In treatment and in clinical research with these and other patients with developmental arrest, two findings were immediately and glaringly consistent. The body image and sensory awareness/integration of these individuals had been subjected to the same process of developmental arrest as their psyches. Their body images were disrupted, blurred, distorted, incomplete, or infantile, and often fluctuated with emotional state. Patients with eating disorders, as well as other more severe narcissistic and borderline individuals with whom we have worked clinically, may not experience the distinctness of their bodies or their body boundaries. Lacking this consistent and accurate internal image of their bodies and sense of self, such patients necessarily rely on other people and external feedback and referents to mirror their worth and adequacy. Object and internal image constancy are missing. Often, the manifest symptomatology is the use of body self stimulation to regulate affect, including the use of food, drugs, alcohol, sex, wrist-cutting, exercise, and impulsive or compulsive behavior.

The clinical applications and illustrations are based largely on psychoanalytic and psychotherapeutic work with patients suffering disorders of the self. Additionally, some data were developed by a multispecialty inpatient treatment team working with young adult and adolescent patients. Developmental data and reconstructions emerge from serial projective drawings, psychological testing, individual psychotherapy, dance-movement therapy, videotape analysis and feedback, body image techniques, neurosensory evaluation/integration, sensory awareness work, family history and family therapy data, biofeedback, and psychodrama.

The central thesis of this book is that an individual's healthy, mature sense of self contains, at its core, a cohesive, distinct, and accurate body self. Compromise of this development can result in arrest as early as the first weeks or months of life, when the nascent sense of self emerges from mirroring experiences with the mother and can extend in changing form throughout development. In affected individuals, these preverbal experiences in the first year of life may fail to acknowledge and confirm a body self separate from the mother, resulting in an incomplete or distorted body self and image, failed in its integration with the psychological self.

This thesis implies that issues involving body self pathology must be addressed and integrated with issues involving the psychological self as a necessary component for recovery from more pronounced narcissistic pathology. The development of body self as a foundation for the sense of self is conceptualized in the first section of this book.

Body self and its derivative representation, body image, are fluid and dynamically interconnected with the psychological self and its derivative representation, self-image. The increasing distinctness of body boundaries and image and the development and maturational complexity of the individual contained within those body boundaries are mutual, complementary, and integrative processes. The first two chapters outline early developmental sequences in the formation of body self and psychological self. The pathological manifestations of arrested development, along with illustrative clinical material and integration constitute the middle section. The final section includes discussion of the clinical applications of these principles. The ineffectiveness experienced by these individuals is at the leading edge in both the developmental and psychodynamic scenario of narcissistic pathology, regardless of the manifestations. The therapeutic applications include, necessarily, the understanding and treatment of disorders of the self in which impulsivity and addictions are prominent.

The work presented here is designed to broaden the applicability of treatment to patients not naturally insightful, verbal, psychologically minded, or creative. These deficits are common in patients with eating disorders, including those who suffer significant narcissistic psychopathology. The body self and body image as basic foundations for a psychological sense of self are developmentally important to all individuals seen in therapy, even those with more developmentally advanced psychopathologies.

This therapeutic framework is organized around a common therapeutic thread, the perspective of empathic listening. From this stance, the therapist listens from within the patient rather than as an observer. The focus is on the patient's internal experience, his or her emotions, perceptions, ways of thinking, and causal explanations, the individual's entire experience. Empathy becomes a bridge of understanding between patient and therapist, the echo in one of the voice in another. Through this process, a patient can ultimately achieve empathy with himself and regulate his own sense of self.

The material concerning the parallel development and integration of body self and psychological self is a precursor to existing psychoanalytic and developmental theory on the sense of self. This developmental line begins with the earliest awareness of body self via empathic merger with and mirroring by the mother and culminates in evocative memories of specific and distinct internally regulated body and self images as the individual's neurophysiological and emotional structures mature.

Section I
Development

1

Developmental Origins
of the Body Self

BODY SELF AND PSYCHOLOGICAL SELF AS
AN INTEGRATED LINE OF DEVELOPMENT

The body and its evolving mental representation are the foundation of a sense of self. Freud recognized the ego as first and foremost a body ego: bodily experiences are the center around which the ego is developed (1). Since Freud's notion of the body ego, the consensus of most developmentalists is that the body self refers to the full range of kinesthetic experiences on the body's surface and in its interior, and the body's functions (2, 8). Fenichel (9) indicated in psychoanalytic writings four decades ago that

> in the development of reality, the conception of one's own body plays a very special role. At first there is only the perception of tension, that is, of an "inside something." Later, with the awareness that an object exists to quiet this tension, we have an "outside something." One's own body becomes something apart from the rest of the world and thus the discerning of self

from nonself is made possible. The sum of the mental representation of the body and its organs, the so-called body-image, constitutes the idea of "I" and is of basic importance for the further formation of the ego.

Lichtenberg (2, 3) describes the concept of the body self as a combination of the psychic experience of body sensation, body functioning, and body image. He hypothesizes that reality testing occurs in a definite developmental sequence of increasing awareness and integration of body self. Since the first reality is body experience, that reality is dependent on what is perceived.

With the exception of the studies of Stern (4) and the clinical-theoretical integration of Lichtenberg (2), published neonatal studies do not speak of body image, of body or self schema. The conceptual language of most early developmental studies is biological and the hypotheses encompass an interactional model; neither language nor conceptualization address the role of internal experience.

What is "reality" for the infant? How does the infant experience the mother? The answer appears to be, at first, by sensorimotor perception of the mother's physical ministrations and responses to the infant's body.

The mother feeds, responds visually and vocally. She responds to a cry with a touch, with a smile to an expression of pleasure, and encourages the infant to respond pleasurably in response to her cue.

Bodily experiences and sensations, internal and surface, form the core around which the ego develops. As the kinesthetic body boundaries are being determined, an important parallel process occurs with psychic boundary formation and functioning.

The subjective reality testing of what is inside and outside the body has its psychological counterpart in the distinction between self and nonself. Accurate, consistent perceptions of body self, psychological self, and their integration, are necessary to a cohesive sense of self.

The sense of self is a balanced blend of all elements of self-experience (10). If components of the self experience are omitted, the psyche mobilizes a restorative or compensating effort, engendering various manifestations of psychopathology. To fully understand the pathology it is necessary to examine the normal developmental elements of body and self awareness.

The infant's body, affects, and movement are initially experienced through the mirroring selfobject. These experiences coalesce into a body self awareness, and then into a body image. The development of an intact body image and physical boundaries, and the subsequent evolution of ego boundaries, represents a continuum. This parallel developmental line of body self and psychological self moves from primary narcissistic fusion/merger states to separation-individuation; from body boundary consistency to ego boundary coherence.

STAGES OF DEVELOPMENT OF THE BODY SELF

The development of a body self can be conceptualized as a continuum of three stages, the first of which is the early psychic experience of the body. The second stage is the early awareness of a body image, with an integration of inner and outer experience. This process forms body surface boundaries and internal state definition. The final stage is the integration of the body self as a container of the psychological self, the point at which the two merge to form a cohesive sense of identity (2).

The Early Psychic Experience of the Body

There is evidence that body experience during the first weeks and months of life is mostly tactile, and only somewhat auditory and visual (6). The awareness of the body based upon tactile sensations is the *first* developmental experience of the body self. The sense of body is the first sense of self, awakened by the mother's touch. The mother relies initially solely on body communication in her relationship with her infant. The mother's hands establish the first body boundary; auditory and visual stimuli have an important but relatively less significant role in the process at this time.

The mother's hands outline and define the original boundary of the body's surface; they describe a shape of which there was no previous sense. Definition and delineation are provided to the infant's otherwise shapeless and boundless space.

The baby is held, wrapped, touched, and supported. The boundaries thus defined have many qualities essential to the developing sense of self, including firmness, gentleness, specificity, consistency, and predictability. Should one or several of these qualities be absent or uncommunicated, or if there is overstimulation or understimulation, body self distortions or nonformations begin, and may later result in narcissistic disturbances.

Kestenberg emphasizes the rhythmic movement between mother and child and the match in movement styles as a foundation in the bond between them and as a catalyst for the infant's development (11). Related to this emphasis, Mahler and Furer (12) have indicated that the earliest sense of "self" is experienced through sensations from within one's body, especially proprioception. These sensoriperceptive stimuli enable the infant to discriminate the body self-schema from its surroundings (12).

Spitz observed the baby's inclination to concentrate on the mother's face, and particularly on the eyes during periods of feeding (7). He demonstrated that during the first five months the normal nursing infant looks neither at the mother's breast nor at her body, but at her face.

The infant's innate tendency is to seek out the mother's gaze, which he does consistently and for extended periods (8). The mother usually engages in the eye-to-eye contact, frequently changing expressions, vocalizing, and generally connecting with the infant in mutual gazes, vocalizations, and movements (8). The mother's resonance with the infant's experience provides him with a "mirror" that reinforces and affirms the infant's sense of existence. This mirroring experience begins the infant's perceptual existence, and from it he develops schemes of the human face, voice, and touch, which subsequently become the matrix for an internal composite experience of the caretaker. At a few months of age, an initial representation of the mother develops from consistent experiences. Soon, the representation can be internally evoked without the other's presence (4). Each consistent experience contributes itself to a more durable representation.

When the baby looks into the mother's face, he sees himself (10). If the mother is empathically aligned with the baby, this is the baby's first experience of effectiveness: his affect produces a mirrored response in the mother. Mutually and reciprocally, the infant's internal state is also given form and definition by the accuracy of this empathic attunement.

The *accuracy* of the mirroring is crucial, because it is the initial linking of mind and body experiences. If the mother does not mirror the infant accurately and consistently, the basis for a mind-body division is formed, inhibiting one's ability to "see the world feelingly," as does Gloucester in *King Lear* (IV.6.151).

The infant has as yet no internal point of reference from which to distinguish between internal experience and the mother's response. The mother's response is reality; she is experienced as an accurate mirror of the infant's response. It is typically not until some time during adolescence (or later) that most individuals come to question whether parents are indeed accurate mirrors of experience, value, and worth.

The mother's influence on the child during earliest development is internalized without language or conceptualization. This preverbal foundation of experience is not available to memory.

The infant's first awareness of self from parental mirroring has been widely investigated (6, 8, 10, 12, 13). Parents in every culture engage in mirroring behavior with the newborn, imitating facial expressions, gestures, and vocalizations. Emde (13) suggests that this is the infant's chance to control parental behavior, to be *effective* in determining something—to be a cause. The Papouseks (14) see parental echoing at two to three months evolving into the parents' actually forming words from the infant's babbling (e.g., "ba-ba" becomes "baby"). Through these words, which usually refer to the self, the infant learns that he is treated and labeled differently from mother, father, sibling, or object; he becomes an individual with distinctness and a name of his own. This is the first objectification of a body self.

There are necessary neurophysiological components to the formation of the body self. First, of course, is an intact sensory system, then the ability to distinguish one's own body from the body of another. The Papouseks (14) have demonstrated that touching something else is perceived differently than touching one's self or being touched. This ability, crucial in distinguishing one's body from another, is necessary in the psychological evolution of self/other differentiation. There is afferent and visual feedback from one's own movement, which is also experienced differently from another's movement. This concept is illustrated by such rare phenomena as individuals with congenital absence of sensation, one case of which is described in the *Psychoanalytic Study of the Child* (15). For this man (now adult), there remains no ability to distinguish body self or body boundaries; he possesses no tactile capacity to know where he ends and others begin. The basis of his psychological self-development was limited, as there was no body self to be its container.

The mother's earliest empathic responses are expressed in following the infant's affective states with gesture, touch, gaze, and voice. Affect as well as kinesthetic sensation, movement, and gaze become a part of shared experience. Communication is multimodal and multisensory. Throughout the preverbal and early verbal period, empathic parents establish patterns of response to all modes and senses of infant communication. If there is an incapacity for empathic attunement or an absence of interest, responses may be limited to only one modality, such as to only distress caused by physical pain. This limited kind of response to a preverbal infant communicates that pain is a prerequisite to soothing attention.

Normal development is characterized by a progressively more complete, integrated body schema from infancy onward. Self awareness incorporates the awareness of one's own body as well as the perception of another's responses to it (16).

The psychic experiences that recognize and register physical function require time-appropriate stimuli for development (1). The need for both specific and time-appropriate stimuli has been confirmed by developmental research on infantile deficiency states (3, 4). The "reality" of this very early infantile stage is the psychic experience of the body. If there is a failure to vividly experience and strongly sense the body, or if the stimuli are insufficient, the psychic experience of the body remains undeveloped and undifferentiated.

There is no available sense of reality in the absence of an internal experience of a body self as mirrored by the responding mother. Throughout life, the intensity of an experience can create a sense of reality, as exemplified by the phantom pain of the amputee, or a dream in which the images and feelings are so intense that they seem real.

In normal development, psychic representations correspond with bodily experiences, to create accurate internal, external, and psychic perceptions. A multitude of isolated and fragmented bodily experiences can thereby become integrated over a period of time in early childhood. Inherently fragmented and unrelated sensations and experiences, such as feeding, hunger, distension, and touch, become integrated into a cohesive body schema and image correlated with psychic representations.

Glover (17) and Spitz (7) refer to separate "ego nuclei" that develop in conjunction with early infantile needs. These ego nuclei become the first organizing or integrating attempts that combine somatopsychic representations.

Definition of Body Surface Boundaries and
Distinction of the Body's Internal State

Empathic parental mirroring molds internal and body surface sensations into distinct and coherent functions of the self. By distinguishing inner and outer, a demarcation is drawn between body boundaries, while a parallel coherent reality of internal body functions and needs independent of the selfobject is developed. The individual develops criteria for identifying the limits of the body self, where one's body ends and the rest of the world begins. Brief absences from the need-satisfying object can occur, as can temporary suspensions of empathic contact, as the infant gradually learns to tolerate incomplete satisfaction of his needs by the mother. Because there is only a functional merger between mother and infant, frustrated need satisfaction forces recognition of the distinctness of body boundaries, and an early sense of the separateness of one's psychic self.

Prolonged physical or empathic absence of the caregiver, characterized by inconsistencies of response for failure in the mirroring function, may lead to denial, splitting, or defensive fusion, with resultant distortions of body self and subsequent ego development. Concurrently, body boundaries may not be distinguished, resulting in a failure to develop cohesive recognition and distinction of internal states.

Symptoms may emerge as distorted efforts to unconsciously reconstitute early deficits. Symptom pictures may be of the sort that promotes awareness of internal states. These include eating disorders organized around basic body functions of eating and elimination and associated physical sensations, such as the distention and fullness that follow bingeing, the elimination that follows laxative or diuretic use, or the vomiting that follows induction of gastric spasm. Alternative symptom pictures may be of the sort that attempt to define the body surface. These may include such activities as wrist cutting, the wearing of heavy loose clothing to stimulate the skin, preoccupation with textures, yearning for and fearing the touch of another, or compulsive weight-lifting to distinctly outline the body muscle mass.

In normal development, experiences achieve an increasing coherence; the need for greater intensity is replaced by greater discrimination and internal clarity. Outer boundaries of the body become more specific, delimited, and easier to distinguish from everything external.

This stage of development, beginning at a few months and extending into the toddler phase, is characterized by a sense of reality based on an integrated body self emerging from newly discovered body boundaries and establishing body states.

Winnicott also emphasizes the importance of the mother's role in body self development. Through adequate handling, the infant comes to accept the body as a part of the self and to feel that the self dwells in and through the body (10). Winnicott agrees with Mahler and other developmentalists that the boundaries of the body provide the limiting membrane between what is "me" and what is "not me," and that the consistent, sensual holding and handling of the infant promotes the child's experience of himself as a unit rather than as a collection of parts. This sense of oneness is essential to ego integration, later physical coordination and grace, and the ability to experience pleasure in bodily activity. The mother is viewed as a "facilitating environment" for the child's critical developmental passages.

If the individual components and nuclei of development are not integrated, conditions exist for pathological maturation. The noninte- grated elements appear as pathological distortions of healthy develop- ment, caricaturing the relationship between the reality of the body self and the developing sense of self. Some symptoms, such as psy- chophysiologic disturbances, indicate various loci of these pathologi- cal nuclei. They are attempts to integrate or heighten awareness of missing developmental experiences and stabilize the overall sense of reality and of self.

The representation of body self evolves into a consistent and coher- ent body image, with increasing clarity of boundary and content. The body image is a complex evolving formulation of an evocative mental representation of the body. Its developmental maturity is based on an individual's formation and perceptions of a series of internal and external stimuli.

Body experiences start to become coherent in the first months of an infant's life as awareness of the internal and surface aspects of the body increases. During this time the infant also develops the first capacity to form mental images. Neurobiologists speak of the physio- logical and anatomical substrates of images, including image forma- tion. Horowitz (18) distinguishes between forming an image (as it is produced in the psychic system) and perceiving an image (as it is derived from external visual stimuli).

During the first weeks and months of life, at those times when the mother is physically absent, so apparently is her image. Only later is an imaging capacity developed that can sustain the representation of the mother beyond her immediate presence.

An infant's imaging capacity begins at Piaget's Stage IV: 8–13 months, at which time the image and its properties seem to exist independently of the object or person perceived (2). As the capacity to make images and internal representations develops, people or objects can exist apart from the infant's sensory perception of them. This imaging capacity is initially primitive and is limited to identifica- tion of symbols of transitional objects: a thumb to suck rather than a breast; a blanket to rub rather than the mother's skin.

The first symbols and the first transitional objects are those repre- senting the body of the mother. The very first transitional object is food, passed from mother to infant. Before their imaging capacity forms, infants do not distinguish objects such as mother, toy, hand or toe from their activities with that object (2). The object is perceived as an extension of their activity.

With the achievement of imaging capacity, the infant comprehends the distinctness of body and object, and develops an awareness of space beyond the body. From these faculties emerges the sense that the infant creates his own image and thereby his own action. The infant distinguishes between his own body and the body "out there"—his image. The toddler thus seems to recognize that the mirror imparts information about his own body and his own actions in a distinct and objectifiable manner, and the movement of that image is created directly by his own actions.

These events in the process of self-discovery are major developmental milestones. The discovery of the body self and of self-determined action confirms and validates a new internal center of initiative.

The individual develops a full imaging capacity at about 18 months, corresponding with Piaget's description of object permanence. By this time the toddler can extend his conceptual capacity beyond himself to include the body of others: for example, drinking from his cup and offering a drink from the cup to a parent or doll (19, 2).

The imaging capacity provides for the evolution from recognition memory to evocative memory. With the development of recognition memory and imaging capacity, object relationships are no longer confined to the infant's immediate action.

Through the period of 13 to 18 months an object must be reexamined and verified (recognition memory). After about 18 months of age, the toddler is able to evoke an image of the absent object and pursue it without any immediate perceptual cues (evocative memory) (20).

Other behaviors, such as response to photographs of the parents and recognition of different photos of mother and father, confirm this maturation of imaging capacity to include evocative memory and more discreet symbol formation during the second year of life.

Through this process, the mirror exemplifies the existence of a separate external world, conveying information and signals about the actions of the infant's body. Ultimately the mirror is used to confirm the ability of the evolving body and psychological self to initiate action. The initiative to act and affect others is increasingly perceived by the toddler as residing within himself. This growth into secondary process and symbolism allows linkage of cause and effect, a higher level of affective and cognitive organization, and ultimately the capacity for fantasy and metaphor.

The self "out there" in the mirror is responded to, usually by 9 to 12 months of age, with delight, action, laughter, and gestures. Between 9 and 12 months of age, infants do not respond differently if the mirror is distorted; in one experiment, toddlers did not notice a label placed on their foreheads (2). Their action response to the mirror is like any other action response to such new experiences, like a mobile, cartoon, or toy.

Between 13 and 15 months the toddler begins to react differently to the mirror. He becomes serious, looks questioningly, and is less active when confronted with his own image. He becomes disturbed with a distorted mirror, notices a label placed on his forehead and reaches for it in the mirror (2). He makes conspicuous movements and gestures in the mirror, and gazes intently at the image. Apparently using his imaging capacities, he sees the image in the mirror as a discrete external entity, which is unconnected to his own body, as exemplified by his reaching for the label in the mirror, rather than reaching for it on his forehead.

The formation of a three-dimensional image of the body is an important element of early ego formation (21). The way one perceives, structures, uses, and moves with one's body is a determinant of inner reality.

First, the body self is the *function* of another. Next, it is immediate, felt *experience:* the emerging extension experience of unsatisfied need. Next, the body self is *form*, objectively distinct patterns of behavior, as well as the subjective and systematic experience of reality. Finally, it is *concept*, a relatively enduring internal frame of reference, comprised of bodily and emotional images, concepts, and experiences. The quality of relative stability over time constitutes the aspect of identity. The metaphors that characterize everything from style to defense, as well as metaconcepts such as "self," are aspects of the self concept. As a concept, the self is a fiction, but not a myth.

The Definition and Cohesion of the Body Self as a Foundation for Self-Awareness

A new level of organized self-awareness begins at about 15 months. This is confirmed by observational studies of the infant discovering himself in the mirror at 15 to 18 months (13), and by the acquisition of the semantic "No." The capacity for and function of "No" is defined by Spitz (16) as evidence of the emerging distinctness of the "I" and "Non-I." Autonomy and self-awareness are emerging. "No" encapsulates developmental statements that: "I am not an extension of you and your body or your desire; this is where you end and I begin—my body is mine and mine alone."

Beginning at 16 to 18 months, infants discover that they are what creates the image in the mirror. They reach for the label on their own forehead (22) and reach to touch a smudge placed on their own nose rather than the image in the mirror (23).

Mahler and Furer (12) and Piaget (24) agree (from different theoretical vantage points) that in normal development a cognitive sense of separate existence and of body self can exist by 18 months. Exploration and familiarity with body parts have already begun by this age.

In normal development the experiences and images of the inner body and the body surface become organized and integrated into an experiential and conceptual whole. They are felt as a coherent unit of body self, which becomes integrated and accepted uncritically as a higher-order self experience uncluttered by nonintegrated components.

Consolidation of a stable, integrated, cohesive mental representation of one's body is a key developmental task during this period. This entails delineation of what is inside and what is outside, with clear, distinct boundaries. Internal body self awareness and intact internal/external boundaries communicate a removal from others that promotes individual distinctness, mastery, and the experience of effectiveness.

An original developmental failure to integrate, or later *dis*integration of a tenuous coherence, pathologically enhances the experience of these individual components. The initial formation of a healthy body self is prerequisite to the experience of further expansion and cohesiveness of the total sense of self. It also prepares the individual for the experiences of continuity and consistency within the body and psychological self despite changes in external environment and circumstances. The integration of inner and outer body and the synthesis of the body self and psychological self provide the basis for further discrimination and development. This constitutes the entire process of information and reality perception.

The body self experience, body images, and self images cohere to form the sense of self. This synthesis of body and psychological selves provides a unity and continuity over time, space, and state (1).

The cornerstone of what one perceives as "real" (reality testing) is the experience of one's self as a constant cohesive entity, durable despite external change. This cohesive entity has an ever-increasing capacity to recognize, integrate, synthesize, and organize change (1).

However, when body self experiences and body boundaries are disrupted by external circumstances, coherence, orientation, and consistency can falter. The natural restitutive urge will seek some external focus to restore the damaged properties to stability.

Reflection and symbolic representation become possible around the second year of life (Piaget's Preoperational Period), when dreams, fantasies, and imaginative play become possibilities and serve as means to control affective tensions. The individual develops a capacity for modifying helplessness at one end of the continuum and grandiosity at the other.

Words become attached to the experiences of internal stimuli and autonomic response, constituting basic affect (23–25).

The maturing brain develops increasingly sophisticated cognitive mechanisms. In the preoperational period, beginning at age two and extending until age five to six, the growing capacity for symbolic functions provides for greater complexity in the conception of the self. The brain is increasingly able to create order from a sea of stimuli, if the empathic caregivers have shaped the infant's patterns of response to stimuli with consistent shaping and mirroring.

REFERENCES

1. Freud, S. *The ego and the id* (standard ed., vol. 19) (pp. 12–60). London: The Hogarth Press, 1923.
2. Lichtenberg, J. The testing of reality from the standpoint of the body self. *Journal of the American Psychoanalytic Association, 26:*357–385, 1978.
3. Lichtenberg, J. *Psychoanalysis and infant research.* Hillsdale, NJ: The Analytic Press, 1985.
4. Stern, D. *The interpersonal world of the infant.* New York: Basic Books, 1985.
5. Schilder, P. *The image and appearance of the human body.* New York: International Universities Press, 1956.
6. Shevrin, H., & Toussieng, P. Vicissitudes of the need for tactile stimulation in instrumental development. *Psychoanalytic Study of the Child, 20:*310–339, 1965.
7. Spitz, R. *The first year of life.* New York: International Universities Press, 1965.
8. Faber, M. *Objectivity and human perception.* Alberta, Canada: University of Alberta Press, 1985.
9. Fenichel, O. *The psychoanalytic theory of neuroses.* New York: W. W. Norton & Co., 1945.
10. Winnicott, D. *Playing and reality.* New York: Basic Books, 1971.
11. Kestenberg, J. *Children and parents: studies in development.* New York: Jason Aronson, 1975.
12. Mahler, M., & Furer, M. *On human symbiosis and the vicissitudes of individuation.* New York: International Universities Press, 1968.
13. Emde, R. The prerepresentational self. *Psychoanalytic Study of the Child, 38:*165–192, 1983.
14. Papousek, H., & Papousek, M. Early autogeny of human social interaction. In M. Von Cranach, Foppak, W. Loepenies & D. Ploog (Eds.), *Human ithology.* Cambridge: Cambridge University Press, 1979.
15. Dubovsky, S. & Grogan, S. Congenital absence of sensation. *Psychoanalytic Study of the Child, 30:*49–74, New York: International Universities Press, 1975.
16. Spitz, R. *No and yes.* New York: International Universities Press, 1957.
17. Glover, E. *On the early development of mind.* New York: International Universities Press, 1956.
18. Horowitz, M. *Image formation and psychotherapy.* New York: Jason Aronson, 1983.
19. Nicolich, L. Beyond sensorimotor intelligence: Assessment of symbolic maturity through analysis of pretend play. *Merrill-Palmer Quarterly, 28:*89–99, 1977.

20. Fraiberg, S. Libidinal object constancy and mental representation. *Psychoanalytic Study of the Child*, 24:9–47. New York: International Universities Press, 1969.

21. Stechler, G. & Kaplan, S. The development of the self: A psychoanalytic perspective. *Psychoanalytic Study of the Child*, 35:85–106. New Haven: Yale University Press, 1980.

22. Modaressi, T. & Kinney, T. Children's response to their true and distorted mirror images. *Child Psychiatry & Human Development*, 8(2):94–101, 1977.

23. Lewis, M. & Brooks-Gunn, J. *Social cognition and the acquisition of self.* New York: Plenum Press, 1979.

24. Piaget, J. *Play, dreams and imitation in childhood.* New York: Norton, 1945.

25. Demos, V. Affect in early infancy: Physiology or psychology. *Psychoanalytic Inquiry*, 1:533–574, 1982.

26. Tomkins, M. The quest for primary motives: Biography and autobiography of an idea. *Journal of Personality & Social Psychology*, 41:306–329, 1981.

27. Emde, R. Changing models of infancy and the nature of early development: Remodeling the foundation. *Journal of the American Psychoanalytic Association*, 29:179–219, 1981.

2

Body Self to Psychological Self

DEVELOPMENTAL BRIDGES

The first reality is the reality of the body. Motor activity is the first mechanism with which reality is tested: whatever can be touched in the external world is real. Reality is persistently influenced by the present, past, conscious, and unconscious images of one's body self (1). The body is the primary instrument through which we perceive and organize the world. We regularly return to the body as a frame of reference throughout development. Subsequent learning and experiences are referred to what has already been sensorily experienced for confirmation and authentication (1). The first symbols and metaphors refer simultaneously to the body and to the outside (nonbody) world.

The special emotional significance with which each individual infuses elements of external reality is often associated with an object's or event's representation of a body part or function. The mother is first experienced as an extension of the infant's body, function, and needs—all of which are perceived as one at this stage of development. The mother exists as a holding environment to meet the infant's needs in a way so unobtrusive that the infant does not experience his needs as needs (2). When the mother is empathic and regularly present there is no need as yet to form symbolic representations of her.

Spitz (3) found that the infant's beginning awareness of "I" and "not-I" is evident at three months. At this time, the infant is able to suspend the urge for immediate gratification and perceives the mother's face and reacts to it, thus becoming aware of the "otherness of the surround."

BEGINNINGS OF MASTERY AND EFFECTIVENESS

When the baby looks in the mother's face, he sees himself (4). If the mother is empathically aligned with the baby, this is the baby's *first experience of effectiveness,* of seeing an internal state formed and defined by the accuracy of the empathic response. *If the mother is not empathically attuned there is no sense of consistent effectiveness and no experience of mastery.*

The first demonstrable desire for mastery occurs at three to four months of age. The superordinate stirring that leads to actualization of the infant's full and true potential has been termed "effectance pleasure"—pleasure in being a cause (5). The Papousecks (6) have demonstrated that beginning as early as four months of age the infant's basic motivation is to function effectively. With particular patterns of head movement, four-month-old infants could activate a light display. The results demonstrated that infants experience pleasure in actively determining the visual stimulation. As the infants eagerly repeated their movements to trigger the lights, they watched the visual display less and less: the pleasure and impetus to repeat the movement appeared to be associated with the *effectiveness* of their action rather than with the actual outcome. The infants seemed to respond positively to solving a problem and especially to having some congruence between their plan or expectation and the ensuing real events. The clinical importance of this principle—the motivation to be effective even if the result is detrimental—will be expanded in chapter 8.

Kestenberg's early child development studies yielded films that show that babies, as early as three months old, exhibit awareness and pleasure in producing marks on a paper with paint brushes and paint (7).

Piaget notes that an accidental action leading to a consequence will be repeated to bring about the consequence (8). The scope of this desire for mastery over the external environment has been further explored by Demos (9), who demonstrated that the goal or consequence that the infant attempts to achieve also includes the reconstruction of an *internal affective state*, rather than just an external event.

The remarkable aspect of these experiments is the demonstration of a *motivation for mastery*—to actively and effectively determine an outcome. The desire for effectiveness and, broadly, for competence, becomes a factor in psychic development as early as four months of age. The infant's basic goal is to function competently. The establishment of contingent control over external and internal events is the infant's basic reward.

As much as infant research has largely neglected the motivation for competence and pleasure in being a cause, psychoanalysis and psychoanalytic therapy have neglected this basic motivation as well. The normal as well as pathological development of this basic motivation for mastery of one's body, emotions, and environment deserves particular attention.

Lichtenberg (10) demonstrates that infants want to learn, perform, master, and experience pleasure at mastery. Their desire for effectiveness and an increasing sense of control changes in form and content from four months and throughout development.

The entire caregiving system, including parents, must continuously adapt to permit the infant's increasing regulatory capacity (9). The system must grant entrance to the newcomer as his own agent. When the caregivers recognize and accept the infant's need and ability to independently affect events, they provide the conditions that establish the infant's capacity for self-awareness, and ensure that an awareness of self will be the basic referent as he organizes his behavior. The child will be able to appreciate what behaviors lead to what states. This self-initiated goal realization will be experienced as the infant's own.

The role of the caregiver in nurturing the developing child's internal regulatory capacities must be ever-changing in content while consistently empathic in process. It is systems training, teaching competence in organizing and regulating one's own behavior in order to achieve goals. The experience of effectiveness is central. The caregiver facilitates goal realization and provides conditions conducive to the child's initiation of goal-organized behavior throughout the developmental spectrum. These behaviors become more complex and sophisticated during the process of development, and the caregiving system must be prepared to permit as well as to promote the persistent broadening of the child's organizing capacity.

THE BRIDGE BETWEEN "SELF" AND "OTHER": POTENTIAL SPACE AND THE TRANSITIONAL OBJECT

At about four months of age, and with the attainment of a capacity for mastery and satisfaction with one's own effectiveness, comes an early awareness of frustration and consequent separateness (4). When the mother is empathic, the infant begins to experience her response to the affects and action he *originates*. He simultaneously experiences feelings of frustration, because the mother is not an absolute extension of his body, his needs, his wishes. The frustration of some of his desires is inevitable and, when well-timed and carefully titrated by the caregiver, it encourages development of frustration tolerance and facilitates symbol formation.

Winnicott proposes (4) that in a well-functioning system of mother-infant unity, the potential space between them is occupied by a state of mind that recognizes the paradox that mother and infant are simultaneously one (in function) and two (as entities).

This unity in healthy development involves the establishment of a capacity for psychological oneness and separateness that creates and informs the other. The infant thus develops the capacity to be an individual in the presence of the mother (11). Touching, looking, smiling, and holding are all reciprocal mother-infant soothing functions. This is a developmental step from the earlier sense of symbiotic merger without potential space or boundaries, a progression from oneness to a distinction between mother and infant. Although this progression is mediated by carefully modulated episodes of frustration (that is, no mother could or should be a perfect extension of need-meeting function), the caregiver's actual intention is the empathic fostering of the child's desire for increasing effectiveness, mastery, and self-regulation. The infant becomes aware of both himself and the mother, although the distinction and basic body boundaries are not yet clear and consistent. Restoration of the lost function (the merged-with mother) is attempted by the illusion-producing reality of a transitional object. The transitional object becomes, then, the first symbol.

The transitional object can be used initially to effect this separation, by being a simultaneous symbol of the mother and a symbol of separateness. The transitional object is a symbol for "separateness in unity, unity in separateness." The transitional object is at the same time the infant (the omnipotently created extension of himself) and not the infant (an object he has discovered that is outside of this omnipotent control) (2).

Food can be recognized as the first transitional *object*. Food is the extension of the mother's body (breast), conveyed as nurturance, emotionally and physically, to become part of the infant's body. Other transitional objects are a part of the infant's body (his thumb), or represent the mother's body (a blanket caressed as the mother's skin).

The distance between symbol and symbolized, mediated by an experiencing self, is the space in which we are other than reflexively reactive beings. This is another "potential space" (11). The infant becomes the creator and interpreter of his symbols, the bridges across this (potential) space.

The early separation of the symbiotically fused infant promotes awareness of self and nonself, and generates a symbol of the selfobject. This developmental advance enables the child to begin internalizing the soothing function previously supplied solely by the selfobject. The symbol is the active creation of the infant. It is his very own, first omnipotently constructed illusion of control over an external selfobject.

The process of symbolization has been described as a restitutional phenomenon aimed at preserving and/or recovering a lost object (12). This formulation is based on conflict theory and is stated in terms of defensive operations and full object differentiation. When the infant is first able to use a symbol, however, object differentiation is rudimentary and incomplete. A developmental approach might reframe the use of a symbol as a step in the abstraction and internalization process toward self constancy and cohesiveness, toward self and object differentiations (13).

The dialectical process (i.e., of a "me" and "not-me") involves two opposing concepts that create, inform, preserve, and negate each other: each stands in fluid relation to the other (14). Although this dialectical process moves toward integration, each integration creates a new dialectical opposition, a new dynamic tension (2), and finally the sense of subjectivity from which self-awareness emerges.

Self-awareness begins in the infant's discovery of himself through what he sees reflected in his mother's responses (4). Self-awareness thus begins with an awareness of *body* experience, sensations, and physical presence. The evolution of self-awareness progresses from reflexive reactivity to the experience of "thinking one's thoughts and feeling one's feelings" (2), and ultimately to intentional self-reflection.

This process facilitates self-awareness (subjectivity), the connection of meaning to experience and then to understanding (objectivity). The (pathological) opposite is an equation of experience with action—the object reflexively acted upon (2) when urge and action are fused without intermediating evaluation. This is another level of potential space: a distance between urge and action. Contemplation and judgment reside in this potential space; without it, one is reflexively active, "impulsive."

The experience of subjectivity introduces the experience of objectivity. In these simultaneous processes, there are distinctions between symbol and symbolized, thought and the object of thought, experience and the naming of it, feeling and action, thought and action (14). It is the beginning of a delay between impulse and action.

A person who is interpreting and symbolizing his experience is engaging in subjective as well as objective processes. Both these experiences require intellectual and emotional distance between subject and what is observed (or, symbol and what is symbolized).

The capacity for self-observation is predicated on an internal construction of the self as observer and as an object of observation. This construction depends on self-awareness emanating from body awareness.

What is first and most clearly observed is also what was first experienced: the body and bodily sensations. This leads to the more developmentally advanced experience of self, then to more abstract conceptualizations and representations of the self, including body image and self image.

This unity of body and self (body and mind) may suffer developmental interruption or arrest at any point, creating a deficit (nonintegration as opposed to split) in the progression and integration of body self and psychological self.

A PRELIMINARY NOTE ON POTENTIAL SPACE, IMPULSIVITY, AND THE THERAPEUTIC PROCESS

The ability to transcend one's immediate situation is reflected in the capacity for symbolism and reason—the process of standing apart from an object or experience in order to objectify it. Objects of observation may include one's own thoughts, body, or behavior, as well as the actions or appearance of other people.

Bodily awareness and self-awareness both depend upon some capacity to transcend one's body and self in order to observe. Body awareness requires only some potential space for observation; self-awareness requires a capacity for abstraction, since "self" is an intellectual concept rather than a physical construct, like the body and its sensations.

The development of self-awareness provides one with the capacity to objectify one's self and the world, and with the capacity to have and use symbols. To see one's body (and, later in development, one's self) as both subject and object requires a third position: the observer. This capacity to transcend one's situation is inseparable from the capacity for self-awareness. The awareness of one's body and self requires the capacity to stand somewhat apart from that which is being observed, and to view one's body and self in a particular situation or context. From that distance, one becomes able to evaluate subjectively and objectively, to abstract, to reason, and to choose among many possibilities for action.

Judgment resides intrapsychically in this (potential) space between urge and action. The most notable manifestations of developmental arrests are impulse disorders (the fusion of urge and action without a contemplative potential space) and addictive disorders (urge and action directed solely toward supplying the self with affect regulators symbolic of a soothing selfobject—food, drugs, alcohol, money, sex).

The space that potentiates the intrapsychic dialectic is replicated in the relationship between patient and therapist, a collaborative observational effort from opposite ends of a line of sight.

Developmentally analogous to the first caregiver's holding environment and symbiotic union, the union between therapist and patient must be established before the patient can progress to separation and individuation. The therapist must contact the patient empathically *before* the patient can establish himself as observer and subject of his own motivations—and the therapist-patient dyad can become subject and object for mutual observation, experience, and scrutiny. This first step conveying an understanding of the patient's experience is to be, in essence, inside it together and listening from the same vantage point. This need was put most succinctly by one analytic patient, who felt that I missed the mark by not first resonating with her experience before I made an interpretation. She said, "I want you to be where I am. I need to know you can be with me first before I can go someplace new with you."

The failed development of a capacity for physical and psychological self-awareness in an individual results in rigid confinement to one particular emotional and ideational context, which might be clinically referred to as "concrete" or "not insightful." When the freedom to create and design one's world is perceived as absent, the individual typically allows the desires or directives, real or imagined, of others to determine conduct, and responses are limited to pleasing conformity or antagonistic rebellion. Passive, pleasing conformity and active opposition both reflect a diversion of individual freedom, in that both behaviors respond to an external rather than an internal point of reference.

Searles has noted that the initial establishment of symbiotic relatedness is a necessary phase in the psychoanalysis or psychotherapy of *all* patients (15). The patient perceives the contextual unit he shares

with the therapist at a higher level of conceptualization and awareness than the distortions or projections he generates to attempt to
meet his developmental needs.

BODY IMAGE FORMATION

The first awareness is of the body. The first symbol is also of the
body—a part of the oneness of mother and infant and a bridge to
something external: food, a blanket, a thumb. The imaging capacity
of the infant matures, and symbols are used more flexibly and reliably, undergoing refinement into various internalizations, including
the formation of a body image.

Developmental research (16) and clinical observation (17) emphasize the significance of developing boundaries between inner and
outer experience as well as between self and others. It is necessary
for these basic boundary distinctions to be established before the
mental representations of self and other can undergo more complex
differentiation, articulation, coherence, and integration in the developmental process.

What becomes internalized is not the object or its functions but
one's *experience* of and with the object. One uses this experience to
form images and fantasies of internal objects (18).

The developmental experiences of the body self that become represented as body image begin in the first awareness through the mirroring selfobject, evolving in healthy development into a cohesive,
distinct, accurate and consistent evocative image of one's body and its
relationship to its physical surroundings. The body image must
evolve accurately as one's physical body matures, and be integrated in
the development of the psychological self.

The development of self-empathy begins with empathy to one's
own bodily experience (body self). By maintaining distinctions
between the inner and outer body self experiences, the individual
establishes the distinctness of self and other.

This model of body image development (and study of pathological
nondevelopment) is integrated with other developmental functions—
especially, as Freud suggested, of ego and self development. The
principles of therapeutic intervention in disorders with body self

pathology are predicated on knowledge of normal development and potential disruptions, and their symptomatic manifestations.

Analytic literature does not provide a clear or consistent conceptualization of the evolution of body self and image (19, 20). Body image is assumed to be something that one either has or does not have, as if it is fixed and either accurate or distorted (21, 22).

Images are concrete and easily accessible ways to code, store, and retrieve information. The transformation of information into an image is a standard mnemonic device. Visual images are probably the first means of thinking, or information processing. Freud (23) suggested that the earliest thinking in infancy is hallucinatory imagery for transient wish fulfillment. Piaget (24) demonstrated that infants have the cognitive capacity to retain mental images of objects seen and then removed from their view.

Philosophers, including Locke, Hume, and Aristotle, considered images to be the basic elements of thought and the motivational basis of emotion. Hume (25) and, most recently, Horowitz (26) attempted to separate the processes and concepts of images from perceptions.

There appears to be a hierarchy of intellectual mechanisms ranging from images to words, to organizing patterns, to superordinate abstractions and inferences that regulate the entire experience of the self.

Some people characteristically use visual images more than others. Bandler and Grinder (27) characterized the three commonly employed representational models as auditory, visual, and kinesthetic. Others (e.g., 26) do not find that individuals can be reliably identified as operating with a specific mode and believe instead that few persons habitually think in only one mode.

Schilder (29) characterizes the evolution of thinking as an advancement from images to symbols and concepts with less sensory quality.

This evolution in cognitive capacity parallels the changing image of the body and the growing ability to abstract the concepts of body self and emotional self.

Self boundaries are presaged by body boundaries; the intactness of both are related. The developmental nonformation or regressive indistinctness of both body and self boundaries in pathological psychic states are elements of this same process in its dysfunctional state.

A body image projective drawing or internal image at any point in time is an arbitrary slice from the ongoing process of maturation, as one's body image slowly evolves from birth to death.

The body self seems to consist of a group of images that are dynamically and preconsciously centered on body experiences. A body image is a conceptual composite from all sensory modalities; the individual's sense of cohesion is also a conceptualization, because the entire body cannot be simultaneously visualized nor can all images/sensations be simultaneously retrieved from memory. In addition to the mental representations, later developmental influences include the reactions of others to one's appearance. Usually preconscious and uncritically internalized, they are not as static as the term "image" might imply. One's body self and body image are developmental processes undergoing gradual maturational change with a cohesive core, analogous to an intact psychological self.

It is only when pathology is introduced in this process that change becomes abrupt, symptomatic, and prominent.

When a body image has been insufficiently formed to sustain the stresses of developmental maturation, it regresses in response to emotional events, and the self state will display rapid oscillations. When such individuals are in regressed states such as narcissistic rage or depletion depression, their body images oscillate as well. Comparisons with body images drawn at other times show remarkable parallels to emotional states (28); that is, at a time of particular emotional turmoil, their body image becomes more distorted, vague, or regressed. In the course of successful therapy, patient and therapist will see a process of maturation, cohesiveness, and distinctness of body image, which parallels developmental maturation (28).

Body self and its derivative representation, body image, are fluid processes interconnected to the psychological self and its derivative representation, self image. They are mutually complementary.

The accurate empathic mirroring of the entire depth and range of the infant's responses establishes the basis for the subjective experience of the body and self. The imaging capacity is crucial to establishment of the objective experience of the body self (29), and the associated distinctness between self and object.

The emerging capacities to subjectively and objectively experience one's body and one's self—as object and as origin of contemplation—parallel the increasing ability to use symbols.

The enhanced subjective and objective experiences of the body and psychological self support Lichtenberg's concept of the "self-as-a-whole," being an initiator and a director of intentional actions (2).

EROTOGENIC ZONES

By 18 to 24 months of age the process of emerging body experience and body self-awareness has developed to include bowel and bladder awareness. The focus on internal body experiences and on the regulation of these boundaries (bowel and bladder sphincter control) further defines internal, external, and the control of passage between the two, and helps to consolidate body image.

Genital awareness, sensation, and exploration also begin at about this time, and further broaden body awareness (30). Galenson and Roiphe have found an increase in genital perineal awareness in boys and girls between 18 and 24 months of age. This awareness follows increased capacity for sphincter control and increased anal and urethral sensation. The associated exploratory activity is less related to excitement than to proud exhibitionism (8).

The physiological consolidation of these sensations promotes a desire to explore, to exhibit one's self, and to be looked at, admired, and affirmed. A painfully negative self-consciousness may result from parents' disapproving regard at this time (31). The caregiver's response to exhibitionistic behavior is crucial in determining whether affirmation/integration or shame/segmentation will predominate in the infant's self image.

The focus and experience of the infant or toddler is much more body-oriented than the adult's. The child is said to live in his body; the adult lives in his mind.

Early developmental milestones are characterized by greater separation from the mother, increasing clarity of self boundaries and of body boundaries, greater integration of body and psychological self, and initial experiences of one's self as the origin of action and intention. The individual grows from undifferentiated to symbiotic to a differentiated state—all in the context of maturing, ever-changing selfobject relationships.

With the beginning of concrete operations at approximately age six, logical thought, a true separation of self and object, and a more discrete, complete body image become possible.

REFERENCES

1. Rose, G. *The power of form.* New York: International Universities Press, 1980.
2. Ogden, T. On potential space. *International Journal of Psycho-Analysis, 66*:129–142, 1985.
3. Spitz, R. *No and yes.* New York: International Universities Press, 1957.
4. Winnicott, D. *Playing and reality* (pp. 1–25). New York: Basic Books, 1971.
5. White, R. Motivation reconsidered: The concept of competence. *Psychological Review, 66*:297–333, 1959.
6. Papousek, H., & Papousek, M. Cognitive aspects of preverbal social interaction between human infants and adults. In Chicago Foundation Symposium, *Parent-infant interaction.* New York: Associated Scientific Publishers, 1975.
7. Kestenberg, J. The use of creative arts as prevention of emotion disorders in infants and children. Presented at National Coalition of Arts Therapy Associations, New York, 1985.
8. Piaget, J. *Judgement and reasoning in the child.* Totowa: Littfield, Adams, and Co., 1959.
9. Demos, V. Affect and the development of the self: A new frontier. Self Psychology Conference, New York, 1985.
10. Lichtenberg, J. *Psychoanalysis and infant research.* Hillside, NJ: The Analytic Press, 1985.
11. Winnicott, D. *Maturational processes and the facilitating environment.* New York: International Universities Press, 1965.
12. Waldhorn, H., & Fine, H. (Eds.).*Trauma and symbolism.* Monograph V. Monograph Series of the Kris Study Group of the New York Psychoanalytic Institute. New York: International Universities Press, 1974.
13. Krueger, D. The "parent loss" of empathic failure and the model symbolic restitution of eating disorders. In D. Dietrich, & P. Shabad (Eds.), *The problems of loss and mourning: New psychoanalytic perspectives.* New York: International Universities Press, 1988.
14. Hegel, G. *Phenomenology of Spirit* (1807). A. V. Miller (Trans.). London: Oxford University Press, 1977.
15. Searles, H. The role of the analyst's facial expression in psychoanalysis and psychoanalytic therapy. *International Journal of Psycho-Analysis, 10*:47–73, 1984.
16. Spitz, R. *The first year of life.* New York: International Universities Press, 1965.
17. Blatt, S. Levels of object representation in analytic and intrajective depression. *Psychoanalytic Study of the Child, 29*:107–157, 1974.

18. Grotstein, J. Perspectives on self psychology. In A. Goldberg (Ed.), *The future of psychoanalysis.* New York: International Universities Press, 1983.
19. Rizzuto, A., Peterson, M., & Reed, M. The pathological sense of self in anorexia nervosa. *Psychiatric Clinics of North America,* 4:471–487, 1981.
20. Button, E., Fransella, F., & Slade, P. A reappraisal of body perception disturbances in anorexia nervosa. *Psychological Medicine,* 7:235–243, 1977.
21. Bauman, S. Physical aspects of the self. *Psychiatric Clinics of North America,* 4:455–469, 1981.
22. Van der Velde, C. Body images of one's self and of others: Developmental and clinical significance. *Journal of the American Psychiatric Association,* 142:527–537, 1985.
23. Freud, S. *The Interpretation of Dreams* (standard ed., Vols. 3,5). London: Hogarth Press, 1964.
24. Piaget, J. *Play, dream and imagination of childhood.* New York: Norton, 1945.
25. Hume, D. Excerpt from "A treatise of human nature." In J. Mandler, & G. Mandler (Eds.), *Thinkings: From association of gestalt* (pp. 51–69). New York: Wiley, 1964.
26. Horowitz, M. *Image formation and psychotherapy.* New York: Jason Aronson, 1983.
27. Grinder, J., & Bandler, R. *The structure of magic: II.* Palo Alto, CA: Science and Behavior Books, 1976.
28. Krueger, D., & Schofield, E. An integration of verbal and nonverbal therapies in disorders of the self: II. National Coalition of Arts in Therapies Association, New York, 1985.
29. Schilder, P. *Mind: perception and thought in their constructive aspects.* New York: Columbia University Press, 1942.
30. Galenson, E., & Roiphe, H. The emergence of genital awareness during the second year of life. In R. Friedman, R. Richart, & R. Van de Wides, *Sex differences in behavior.* New York: Wiley and Sons, 1974.
31. Tomkins, S. *Affect, imagery, consciousness. Vol. 2, The negative affects.* New York: Springer, 1963.

Section II
Psychopathology

3

Pathological Sequences in Body Self Disorders

DEVELOPMENTAL DESCRIPTIONS

Research on deficiency states in infancy has demonstrated that failure to develop a normal psychic representation of the body may result from insufficient intensity of stimulation as well as from cognitive and emotional overstimulation (1–3).

We can now specify more about the quality of selfobject relationships and the resulting psychopathology. Early developmental disruptions in the process of establishing a stable, integrated, cohesive body image seem to result from one or several maladaptive self-selfobject interactions.* To (over)simplify, these early developmental

---

*These conclusions are based largely on psychoanalytic and psychotherapeutic work with patients suffering disorders of the self. Some data were developed by a multispecialty inpatient treatment team working with young adults, adolescents, and eating disorders patients. Developmental data and reconstructions emerge from serial projective drawings, family therapy, psychological testing, neurosensory integration, individual psychotherapy, and dance-movement therapy. In the inpatient setting, specific techniques and studies focusing on body self develop-

pathological sequences fall into three groups. Although not mutually exclusive, the types of interactions can be described as:

1. Overintrusiveness; overstimulation
2. Empathic unavailability
3. Inconsistency or selectivity of response

Overintrusiveness; Overstimulation

Overly intrusive parents attempt to remain merged with their children from infancy onward, disallowing the processes of separation, individuation, and growth toward autonomy. The parent's behavior toward the children is characteristically controlling, protective, and enmeshed, with predominant demands for conformity (4). The body self and image is experienced by these individuals as indistinct, blurred, or easily invaded, and they may attempt to establish a body self and boundary distinctness in such primitive ways as refusing to eat, or exercising to feel physical sensation (5).

When an individual experiences physical and emotional intrusiveness and overstimulation, primitive protective measures may be mobilized, which result in development of a higher threshold to stimuli, a tuning out or withdrawal (6). In infants, this may subsequently interfere with psychic representation at a higher level, affecting integration of physical and psychic representation. The consequent pathology in later life requires that a more intense, more extreme experience is required in order to produce psychic representation or recognition of feeling. Sequelae include such distortions of tactile stimulation as limpness when held, an intense fear of/wish for being touched, a desire/avoidance for physical intimacy, sensations of numbness or somatic inattentiveness, misperceived body image, or preoccupation with textures.

The transsexual male, whose body and psyche were so intermingled with that of his mother that there came to be no somatic or psy-

---

ment include dance-movement therapy techniques, videotape analysis and feedback, body image tracing, clay sculpting of body image, neurosensory evaluation/integration, family history evaluations, and biofeedback.

chic distinction, is an extreme clinical manifestation of infantile over-stimulation (7). This intermingling and continued fusion of the body of both mother and son is illustrated by the report of a transsexual male who recalled that, at approximately age four, he looked at his arms as they were moving and asked, "Are these my arms or are these Mother's?" The mother had carried him and intermingled with him physically to the extent that he had no independent psychic representation of his body or self.

Anorexia nervosa is a more common clinical example of this developmental arrest. The illness is, in part, an attempt to delineate an ill-defined body self and psychological self.

The effects of physical impingement and overintrusiveness are further illustrated by a study of infants who were force-fed by stomach tube. The infants developed a lack of interest and competence in oral intake, had abnormal hunger satiation patterns, and could not recognize internal signals from their bodies (2). As they matured, they lacked motivation, intentionality, vitality, and, especially, a sense of mastery. This affected their activity and vigor in searching, exploring, and mastering various activities, ultimately manifesting in a more passive disturbance of normally active and aggressive patterns.

Lichtenberg (8) has written that,

> These evidences of pathological development of normal psychic body experience in instances of specific stimulation deficiencies and of maternal deprivation indicate that body-self experience (and the nonexperiential body schema) develops normally only when the phase-appropriate intensity of specific stimulation occurs and the affective interchange between infant and mother supports and sustains the body experience.

Intrusiveness upon the privacy of personal and inner space may range from actual invasion of the child's body space: sexual assault, forced feedings or evacuations, or unrelenting body contact; to penetration of the child's emotional world: manipulation of feelings or thoughts, devaluation of attempts at mastery, demands that the child's own perceptions be negated or denied. Families may rationalize intrusive treatment of a child as protectiveness, discipline, or family unity.

In order to experience a stable sense of self, one must first have experienced the integrity of one's own body space and boundaries. It is necessary to have been treated as a distinct entity, beginning with one's body and its relationship to its surroundings.

Empathic Unavailability and Nonresponse

When the parent is unable to empathize accurately and consistently with the infant's internal experiences, responses to emotional and physical experiences, movements, and affects will be incomplete, lacking the infant's experience as point of reference. Body boundaries may not be consistently defined by caress, touch, or secure holding. When these basic experiences are not accurate or consistent, the infant does not develop a reliable experience of internal body sensational affect or of body boundary, and later experiences his body self as incomplete and his body image as distorted. The projective drawings of body image of these individuals are distorted, without shape, with blurred boundaries, and excessively large (5). These are among the clinical features seen in bulimics.

Niederland (9) described a series of artist-patients in psychoanalysis who showed marked changes in body experience and perception, particularly during periods of intense creativity. Each had fantasies of being deficient, incomplete, misshapen, or ugly. During their creative periods, their bodily experience changed to a perception of completeness, wholeness, and freedom from deficiency or inadequacy. When difficulties arose in their creative work, their perceptions of insufficiency and defect returned. These artists' fantasies of incompleteness and deficiency were based in the nonformation of a distinct body image due to early trauma and failure in bonding with their mothers. Niederland cites individual elements of their artistic output in support of his postulations.

Niederland describes the "felt experience of the body" as the sum of the personal, ever-present experiences of kinesthetic-visual-auditory and perceptive-sensorial-emotional-cognitive ego functions.

Physical trauma can also constitute overstimulation. Examples include exposure to sexual or aggressive experiences, child abuse, operations, illnesses, or injuries. One becomes overwhelmed and unable to integrate or to control bodily sensations. During these over-whelming states, there may be a regression to (or, if early enough, nondevelopment beyond) preoccupation with the body self and archaic imagery (10). An example is a young girl who had developed true anorexia nervosa by age eight. Since she was in the middle of her latency stage and was obviously too early for a more typical separa-tion-individuation crisis of puberty, she had suffered numerous body traumas due to medical and surgical invasions of her congenitally malformed genitourinary system. The only area of control of her body that she experienced was to not eat.

Later in development, temporary losses of body control, such as soiling, crying, or even tripping and falling, can create overwhelm-ing feelings of shame and embarrassment. These feelings involving insults to the body self may strain beyond tolerance the sense of self cohesion and body reality, and are often expressed as a desire to escape from one's body or shed one's skin (8).

At times of intense anxiety, an individual's focus of attention shifts from mastery to basic aspects of body self intactness and preoccupa-tions with body sensations, body schema, and body language.

In more developmentally advanced psychopathology there is an integrated body schema, with a specific dynamically significant loss fantasy, such as castration anxiety or immobilization. Fantasies of los-ing vital body parts or functions occur in conjunction with emotion-ally charged relational interactions and events. In those individuals with more structurally intact psychopathology (for example, psy-choneurosis), the fantasies of loss occur without severe threat to a sense of self-cohesion.

More pronounced disturbances in the emergence of body self and psychological self, such as borderline and narcissistic personality dis-orders, occur when the sense of self-cohesion is threatened or has failed to develop. In these more severe states, preoccupation with bodily experience is both a product of fragmented body and psycho-logical selves, and an attempt to establish or restore a body integrity and representation. Such symptoms/restoration attempts may include depersonalization, severe hypochondria, or the somatic delusions of psychoses (11, 12). In these conditions, reality testing of internal ver-sus external experience may be temporarily impaired, indicating a basic nonintegration and distortion of body image, or a regressive segregation of tenuously amalgamated body images, with damage to global self-cohesion and self image.

Inconsistency or Selectivity of Response

Parental response to selective stimuli from the infant creates a selective reality. For example, the mother may ignore affective and kinesthetic stimuli, and respond only to physical needs or physical pain. This response pattern teaches the infant to perceive and organize experiences around pain and illness in order to obtain attention and affection. The affirmation of body self and psychological self through pain and discomfort entrenches itself in personality and characteristic modes of interaction, with a resultant predisposition toward psychosomatic infirmities.

The mother who provides gratification to her child only when he behaves in a dependent and clinging manner enacts another maladaptive pattern of selective response. Emotional approval is withdrawn if this child moves toward separation-individuation. The extreme manifestation of this mode of selectivity is the borderline personality disorder (13).

The formation of a stable, integrated, cohesive mental representation of one's body is central to individual development. This core body self is composed of an accurate, differentiated internal awareness and clear, distinct body boundaries. The conceptualization of an individual internal space emerges simultaneously with the evolving psychological self.

PATHOLOGICAL MANIFESTATIONS AND ATTEMPTS AT RESTITUTION

Disturbances in differentiating self and other affect the individual's ability to create symbols of the body self and the affective self. Distinctions between the symbol and the object symbolized are incomplete; thinking is concrete, without the capacity for abstraction or representation of the body and its contents, including feelings (14).

Lacking a basic distinction between symbols and objects symbolized (mother, self, feelings, etc.), the affected individual must rely upon the immediate experience of her own body to elicit a self representation. The representation of self must be through the body self experience—not through a symbolic representation of the self. Sensorimotor experience of the body self is achieved by inflicting pain, gorging with food, exercising excessively, starving to induce hunger pangs, and otherwise stimulating the body. Food becomes a vehicle (as the razor blade is the vehicle in wrist-cutting) with which to attain a sensory experience. A distinct and complete image of either the body self or the psychological self has never been consolidated. The resultant concrete, nonsymbolic level of operation disallows the psychological distance required for movement beyond a transitional object. *Symbolic equations* rather than *true symbols* predominate (14). Symbolic equations differ from true symbols in that they are seen and experienced as original objects rather than as substitutes or symbols for original objects. With a symbolic equation, there is no "as if" quality. The individual must engage in specific, concrete, body-oriented action or stimulation in order to achieve a representation of the need-meeting object.

The failure to achieve this subjectivity of body self and self experience relates to the inability to symbolize, fantasize, or achieve integrated, change-producing insight. Subjectivity is a reflection of the ability to differentiate symbol, the object being symbolized, and the action creating the symbol (14).

An individual with a defective or incomplete body self (and thus psychological self) is motivated toward completion and restitution of that basic defect. Kohut explained these psychological transactions not on the basis of the underlying fantasy or drive, but on the structural nature of the underlying deficit (11). His formulations were focused on the psychological self, but can be extrapolated to the foundations of body self as well, assisting us to subdivide self-restitutive (or self-*formative*) attempts according to behavior, fantasy, and symptom.

Behavior can be understood through consideration of (1) the nature of the structural deficit and (2) the nature of the solution covering a primary deficit or compensating for a less severe deficit.

Fantasy is the generation of images from a desire for the response that promotes structural integrity.

Symptoms can be viewed as attempted adaptations rather than as expressions of a desire to harm one's self: restitutions of body self integrity and restoration of self-selfobject. Evaluation of the symptom's adaptive function must consider the locus and nature of the symptom and its sequence, the nature of the restitutive attempt, and the state or condition that restitution seeks.

A progressive sequence of disorganization and attempted restitution characterizes distorted or incomplete body self formation, with a resultant compulsive or addictive activity. This activity is usually consistent for a particular individual, a characteristic and recurrent maladaptive behavior, rather than a random variety of symptomatic responses: the bulimic will binge and purge each time she is distraught.

Impulsive behavior typically occurs as a reaction to the narcissistic injury resulting from the change in the individual's relationship with a significant other. The behavior is an attempt to regain control (16). Impulsive action can include binge eating, alcohol and drug abuse, suicidal attempts or gestures, compulsive sexual intercourse, or self-mutilation. The precipitant of a disruption in the connectedness with a selfobject reopens a narcissistic wound. The impulsive act contains a fantasy of restitution either symbolically (e.g., food as nurturance) or directly (e.g., impulsive behavior designed to force a response). Related features include nonintegration of the act's consequences, a focus on guilt rather than a sense of shame and personal disintegration, and attempts to maintain distance from intimates, thereby avoiding the risk of narcissistic injury (16).

The impulsive action adopted as restitution for the disorganization precipitated by a narcissistic injury is typically directed toward the individual's body. The actions are intended to stimulate some part of the body and create an acute awareness of body self sensations. The validating effort focusing on the body is also fulfilling an organizing function for a fragmented or fractured ego by directing focus to the first and most basic organizer of ego experience and structure: the *body ego*.

The individual who engages in this cycle of narcissistic vulnerability, disorganization, and impulsive restitutive attempts typically selects a consistent and characteristic maladaptive response rather than a wide variety of reparative efforts to heal emotional injuries. The bulimic will consistently binge and purge, rather than seek other palliatives for psychic distress.

An understanding of the content and process of impulsive action does not satisfactorily explain the event. Compulsive binge eaters do not eat because they are physically hungry, nor is compulsive sexual activity a response to sexual arousal. The intent as well as antecedent experience are part of the impulsive action. Such impulsive acts as bingeing and wrist cutting are primitive attempts to stimulate a body self experience and representation. The intent must be distinguished from the result. The intent of an anorexic may be to effect separateness, autonomy, and mastery—but the result may be self-destruction. The anorexic's motives may also include interpersonal elements, such as regulating distance in intimate relationships, intrapsychic elements, such as the attempted restitution of a disorganization, and defensive elements, such as disavowal of unacceptable activities and affects. The remnants of magical thinking underlying the restitutive effort, including the disavowal of responsibility inherent in denial, are prominent components. The sense of power associated with impulsive action, as well as the sense of disillusionment and disappointment in the limited scope and durability of the restitutive effort, must be empathically addressed in the therapeutic encounter.

The shift in focus from cognition and verbalization to physical sensation and action is in itself an indication of regression to an earlier point of arrested ego development. The bodily focus of the impulsive act represents a primitive effort to regulate affect and perception by manipulating their presumed physical source. Attempts to decipher the "acting out" of impulsive patients have examined the content and result of their actions, the impulsivity of the actor, or the feelings being avoided by a refocus to the action. Patients themselves will typically identify the intention of impulsive action as an attempt to achieve a notable bodily experience that would reestablish their groundedness in their bodies and thus provide a basis for reorganization at moments of extreme disharmony.

Repetition compulsion, described first by Freud (17) and elaborated by Loewald (18), has different meanings at different developmental levels. At a neurotic level, the compulsion to repeat actions, thought, and situations involves the reenactment of major conflictual life themes in order to achieve a more favorable resolution. One repeats in order to effect mastery. In cases of severe narcissistic pathology, the compulsive repetition of specific behaviors or impulsive actions constitutes what individuals perceive as their most effective effort at reconstituting ego and body integrity following injury to a fragile self. Such individuals are unable to mobilize defensive or organizing fantasies because their body selves have been neither consolidated nor integrated with a psychological self.

Many behaviors regarded as impulsive, addictive, or unrelenting are designed to evoke or establish boundaries. Spending sprees create the illusion of power and limitlessness, but actually tend to enforce concrete limits and powerlessness when money runs out. An argument with an intimate may be designed to establish the presence and the boundary function of that person. The binge eater describes eating to fill feelings of emptiness and despair, to anesthetize herself to emotional pain; her bingeing actually enables her to feel and experience a part of her body as real and to focus the pain in a particular location (her stomach), which she can now master by purging. She thus manipulates a part of her body to focus and alleviate psychic pain. The need for a sense of structure and containment was described by a patient who reported that she felt no boundaries in any activity she pursued. When she exercised, her end point was collapse from exhaustion. When she worked, she would stop only when she could no longer function or concentrate. When taking a multiple-choice test, she always chose the most extreme answer to any question.

One of the difficulties in describing this pathological sequence, as well as in discussing it with patients, is developing a language to do so. It is difficult at best to have a shared language for discussing selfobject functioning and meaning to an individual; language is insufficient to describe some of the experiences of an individual. Not only are many experiences preverbal, but the sequence is not linear. Kohut (11) described fragmentation anxiety, separation anxiety, paranoid anxiety, emptiness, aloneness, existential despair —all of which say much from particular vantage points of experience or observation, but even collectively may not say or be specific enough.

The common theme of these terms is the narcissistic vulnerability of certain individuals, in association with a precipitating interruption in the emotional availability of a significant person (18). This change in the availability or relationship of a significant other can result in the internal experiences of hurt, anger, and disorganization. The narcissistically wounded individual then attempts to control something specific, concrete, and external that directly stimulates some part of the body. This is a dual attempt to regulate the affect of a fragmented sense of self, and to restore selfobject functioning.

Such restitutive and organizing efforts involving bodily experience and perception can also occur when a relationship is experienced as too close or too intimate. The impulsive actions serve to restore a more comfortable distance and an identifiable division between self and other, which restore some perception of body boundary and integrity, and thereby some organization within that reconstructed but fragile boundary. This process is typically seen in couples with indistinct ego and body boundaries who find themselves in an enmeshed relationship. When the degree of intimacy blurs the boundaries between them, one or both may attempt to reestablish some distance, and thereby some distinctness, by precipitating bickering and other forms of discord. The anorexic attempts to establish a boundary between herself and her parents by refusing food, demonstrating where her body begins and where the controlling influence of her parents ends; within this process she is struggling with the shared notion that she is literally an extension of them.

These dynamics can also be designed to reinvolve a member of the family who becomes preoccupied, emotionally absent, or otherwise disengaged. Impulsive acts and other apparently maladaptive efforts sometimes succeed in precipitously engaging the response of uninterested others. These actions, albeit negative, can reconstruct emotional and systemic equilibrium (20, 21).

The disorganizing effects of intimacy are addressed by impulsive actions designed to reestablish boundaries and promote restitution. The boundary-regulating intent and the attempt to compensate for porous, vague, or ineffective body and ego boundaries must be confronted as central issues in therapy, where the result rather than the intent of action can sometimes occupy attention. When the self-destructive result becomes the therapeutic focus, that patient can perceive the therapist as judgmental, critical, or nonempathic. More importantly, the patient may sense that the core of the emotional discomfort has not been approached; the therapist's attempt to confront the problem at the easily accessible superficial (symptomatic) level will usually be no more effective than the patient's.

These patients describe their subjective experience as a feeling of being hopelessly lost, with a sense of *losing form*. Prior to the narcissistic injury, the selfobject had been functioning as a referent and regulator of form and boundary functions, including the experience of body intactness and shape. With the withdrawal, unavailability, or symbiotic enmeshment of that selfobject, the patient precipitously loses a sense of form, because when the selfobject's boundary-regulating function ceases, she must rely solely upon her own vague or unformed body self representation. These indistinct body boundaries seem to represent the most basic level of form and foundation of the self. Their incomplete development can be illustrated by the patient's projective drawings of her own body image (5).

PATHOLOGICAL SEPARATION-INDIVIDUATION: CONTEXTS AND ADAPTATIONS

Delimiting space is an important developmental task of infancy. The process includes differentiating body self from others, differentiating psychological self and selfobject, and consolidating consistent internal representations of self and object. The evolution of these integrated developmental events continues through adolescence, and features expanding bodily/emotional/social space, sexual awareness and modeling, increased separation-individuation, and changing body functions and responses.

Developmental errors at the stage of symbiotic union with the mother may result in fear of losing oneself in another or of being "trapped" by another. An individual arrested at this phase of development will organize relationships around increasing closeness to another, followed by anxiety about loss of self-boundaries, and a subsequent retreat to recreate those boundaries and the (potential) space between the two. Patients typically describe the isolation and loneliness they experience and their retreat to their "own space." This type of developmental arrest results in the need to establish some distinctness, beginning at the most primitive level of separation: body boundary. The failure to initially satisfy the symbiotic needs, through either an inadequately formed or an overintrusive symbiosis, results in a compromised developmental advance, and inadequate body and self boundaries.

If development of a complete and distinct body self is arrested, a later compensatory attempt to supply this experience may employ intense sensory stimulation to provide perceptions of the body: inordinate exercise, induction of physical pain, intense physical stimulation, or extreme physical conditions. At times of emotional stress, there may be regression to the body self. Stimulation and reintegration of the basic body self is the most primitive adaptive attempt at psychic reorganization.

> A 15-year-old girl tried desperately to control her overwhelming compulsion to exercise. She reported that, "I tried and tried not to give in and exercise, but the anxiety was overwhelming. I felt that if I didn't exercise I would lose it—that I would just fade into everyone else—like my body would just become a blob mixed in with everyone else around me. Then I'd be like everyone else—not special". She regressively attempted to vividly reestablish her body self experience and boundaries—to feel real and distinct.

The element of confused separation-individuation was further illustrated by a letter from the parents of a 22-year-old woman hospitalized for treatment of anorexia nervosa. Her mother wrote, "We need to give you our love and receive yours in return. We are all hurting so much. You are and always will be a part of our bodies." In a family therapy session, the mother told the therapist that, "When she left home it was like losing a part of me—like my arm or part of my body. Earlier, I had even tried to eat for her."

Other pathological products of these developmental failures can include intense hallucinations and somatic delusions, which promote a strong but false sense of reality (8). When the internal experiences of body self are not consistently mirrored and accurately validated by the mother, there is no cohesive sense of their reality. Sometimes, the intensity of one's psychological experiences can create its sense of reality, as with the amputee's phantom limb pain, or the dreamer's reorganized world. This capacity for reconstituting experience around emotional or perceptual errors is pronounced in individuals with basic developmental defects.

An early prolonged actual or emotional absence from the nurturing figure may foster a need to tune out or totally extinguish internal reality by denial, splitting, or defensive fusion. The result is distorted ego development. Concurrently, the body boundary may not be adequately developed, resulting in a combined inability to recognize and distinguish either internal or physical realities.

Later attempts at restitution of these early deficits can manifest as psychopathology. Symptoms may include an inordinate need for (and fear of) physical contact, manifesting as hypersexuality without intimacy; wrist slashing in order to feel real and distinguish boundaries; and eating disorders (which describe physical as well as emotional boundaries). Heavy, loose clothing is preferred by some such individuals because of the immediate skin stimulation—the rubbing of the clothes promotes awareness of body surface. We treated an adolescent girl who described an emotional correlative for the feelings her clothing stimulated: "I feel like I'm being hugged." Patients with eating disorders enjoy the illusion of smallness inside large clothes, concealment of the body, and warmth for a hypothermic body. Weight training is pursued by some because of the consequent sharper definition of muscle and body tone, as well as the delineation of body contour and stimulus barrier. Eating disorders are focused in basic body functions of eating and elimination, and concomitant symptomatology may include such external reflections of these internal processes as the use of laxatives, diuretics, or vomiting.

Studies of patients with anorexia nervosa support clinical observations from both individual and family perspectives that families of anorexics have greater boundary difficulties than do other families (21, 22). Sugarman postulates that these boundary difficulties per se become internalized by the anorexic patients (21). Our clinical observations lead us to hypothesize that indistinct, undefined, or intrusive interpersonal boundaries in a family preclude the development of internal boundaries: there are no boundaries to internalize. The process of boundary formation begins with body boundary itself. The symptomatology of anorexia nervosa may be understood as an attempt to create or accentuate boundaries between self and others.

Especially at times of intrusiveness or narcissistic injury, the desire to accentuate the boundary between self and others can lead to social withdrawal and suppression of feelings in order to retain an experience of separateness (22).

A persistent determination to defy the wishes of others is characteristic of this distorted assertion of separateness and independence. The process of separation-individuation, wherein one chooses to no longer function solely as an extension of the feelings and desires of another, begins with opposition. Saying "no" creates a boundary: "no" means "this is where you end and where I begin." In some families where complete reliance on structure and demand for perfection is omnipresent, mistakes are the only thing children can truly call their very own. Whispers of transition in normal separation-individuation become shouts at every juncture in a pathological process. Secrets, which create a potential space between child and parent, are zealously created and maintained; the greater the experience of intrusiveness, the more necessary secrets become.

Without internal referents, one is inclined to compensate by seeking an external explicit metaphor for what is missing within. A discrete, concrete external symbol replaces, rather than merely represents, its vague, fuzzy internal referent. Food and sex, for example, can become concrete metaphors for the internal experience of body self, replacing the provider who would have originally supplied internal nurturance, mirroring, and stimulation.

The individual relying on stimulation, risk-taking activities, physical excitement, and persistent testing of limits and boundaries exemplifies attempted restitutions of inadequately formed and internally regulated self-body experiences and body boundaries. An individual compulsively pursuing various excitement-producing activities attempts to remedy a defect of body self representation and ego functioning. One's sense of the reality of body state and of self-coherence is then continually dependent on that particular intense stimulation.

REFERENCES

1. Shevrin, H., & Toussieng, P. Vicissitudes of the need for tactile stimulation in instinctual development. *Psychoanalytic Study of the Child, 20:*310–339, 1965.
2. Dowling, S. Seven infants with esophageal atresia: A developmental study. *Psychoanalytic Study of the Child, 32:*215–256, 1977.
3. Wolff, P. *The developmental psychologies of Jean Piaget and psychoanalysis (Psychological Issues, Monograph 5).* New York: International Universities Press, 1960.
4. Boszormenyi-Nagy, I., & Spark, G. *Invisible loyalties.* New York: Harper & Row, 1973.
5. Krueger, D., & Schofield, E. An integration of verbal and non-verbal therapies on eating disorder patients. *Arts in Psychotherapy, 13:*323–331, 1987.
6. Demos, V. Annual Self Psychology Conference, New York, 1985.
7. Krueger, D. Diagnosis and management of gender dysphoria. In W. Fann, I. Karacan, A. Pokorny, & R. Williams (Eds.), *Phenomenology and treatment of psychosexual disorders.* New York: SP Medical and Scientific, 1983.
8. Lichtenberg, J. The testing of reality from the standpoint of the body self. *Journal of the American Psychoanalytic Association, 26:* 357–385, 1978.
9. Niederland, W. *Psychoanalytic Quarterly, 45:* 185–212, 1976.
10. Peto, A. Body image and archaic thinking. *International Journal of Psycho-Analysis, 40:* 223–231, 1959.
11. Kohut, H. *The analysis of the self.* New York: International Universities Press, 1971.
12. Kernberg, O. *Borderline conditions and pathological narcissism.* New York: Jason Aronson, 1975.
13. Kinsley, D. The developmental etiology of borderline and narcissistic disorders. *Bulletin of the Menninger Clinic, 44:*127–134, 1980.
14. Segal, H. Notes on symbol formation. *International Journal of Psycho-Analysis, 38:* 391–397, 1957.
15. Segal, H. On symbolism. *International Journal of Psycho-Analysis, 59:*315–319, 1978.
16. Lansky, M. The explanation of impulsive action. *International Journal of Psychoanalytic Psychotherapy* (in press).

17. Freud, S. *Beyond the pleasure principle* (Standard ed. Vol. 18). London: Hogarth Press, 1964.

18. Loewald, H. Some considerations on repetition and the repetition compulsion. *Papers on psychoanalysis*. New Haven: Yale University Press, 1979.

19. Mahler, M. A study of the separation individuation process and its possible application to the borderline phenomena in the psychoanalytic situation. *Psychoanalytic Study of the Child, 26:* 403–424, 1971.

20. Lansky, M. Treatment of the narcissistically vulnerable couple. In M. Lansky (Ed.), *Family therapy and major psychopathology.* New York: Grune and Straton, 1981.

21. Sugarman, A., Quinland, D., & Devenis, L. Ego boundary disturbance in anorexia nervosa: Preliminary findings. *Journal of Personality Assessment, 46:* 455–461, 1982.

22. Sours, J. The anorexia nervosa syndrome. *International Journal of Psycho-Analysis, 55:* 1567–1576, 1974.

4

Psychosexual Manifestations
of Self Pathology

THE BODY SELF AND SEXUAL PERVERSIONS

Psychosexual awareness and experiences serve as psychic organizers to consolidate and complete body awareness, and to consolidate self and object differentiation and representations.

A cohesive, stable, and positively colored self-representation is established through a series of empathic experiences with selfobjects who can be idealized and who can mirror the individual's own worth. If this process is deficient, the individual continues to seek substitutes for missing or defective internal functions to maintain self-cohesion.

For developmentally arrested patients, sexual perversion may be an attempt to experience the early infantile function of body and psychic stimulation, thereby providing cohesion to a crumbling or nonintegrated self-representation (1). For other individuals with higher level (i.e., neurotic) organization, perversions may serve as a regressive defense against oedipal conflict and reassurance against castration anxiety (2).

The narcissistic individual may perceive his own body—or its mirror image—as a sexual object. The focus on his mirror image is an effort to retreat to the body self to restore and stabilize a crumbling self-representation. Even more basic pathology is indicated when an individual is more desperately engaged and persistently preoccupied with body image, attempting to establish a body self and representation.

The earliest manifestations of the sexual perversions are articulated in the language of the patients' bodies, expressing a dual desire for oneness and distinctness. The first interactions of infant and mother occur in affective, motoric, and physical bodily experiences. The infant's experience of deprivation, or intrusion, or an alternation of both, occurs with-in the body. Deprivation, in the broadest sense, is failed empathy: the absence of understanding or response to the infant's needs. Intrusion is characterized by the mother overriding the infant's needs and perceptions and imposing her own upon him.

Narcissistic symptomatology is typified by an attempt to experience a satisfactory selfobject connectedness by the most basic (and, at times, only) source: the physical experiences of the body.

Person (3) suggests that fear of female unavailability, abandonment, and/or personal inadequacy fuels the male fantasy of the omniavailable woman: perpetually aroused, instantly available, perfectly responsive to male desire. This fantasy theme is the female projection of a man's sexual self-image while at the same time a recreation of a continuity with (the oneness of) the preoedipal "feeling" mother, who is an instant and total extension of his wish and desire.

Transvestism

The male transvestite, by entering the woman's (his mother's) clothes, is symbolically entering his mother's body, fusing himself with her. Glasser (4) writes that the transvestite "seeks to *be* her by reinforcing the illusion built on stimulation by believing that he is physically feeling what she feels, as if the arm that feels the sleeve of the blouse, or the shoulders that feel the strap of the brassiere, are as much her arm or shoulders as his." Glasser illustrates this with the example of a transvestite who would never wear his wristwatch, even if hidden from view, so that he might have a complete feeling of unity. The enactment of the bodily and psychic merger is concluded by undressing, emerging into his own distinct body self to complete the scenario. The anxiety of annihilation is resolved in a masterful triumph of separation.

Bodily perceptions are essential to the experience of cross-dressing. The transvestite does not seek to feel like an *actual* woman, but to feel a wholeness and completeness. The transvestite needs to complete a sense of self in order to feel what is missing, the complete unity of oneness. He can then feel that he is emerging whole and intact, separate in the individual manhood represented by his genitalia. The attempt at establishment of wholeness is conducted by manipulating his perception of the body and all its parts.

The following vignette is from an evaluation session with a 41-year-old man, a midmanagement executive with a large company, who came for treatment of his "addiction to sex." His current addiction to sex, predominating his life for the last two years, was only the most recent of a succession of addictions that he recounted: money, food, alcohol, work. He also described prior experiences with cross-dressing, beginning at age 13 and lasting about four years, and for another period between the ages of 20 to 29.

Patient: I remember the pure pleasure of the feeling of cloth against my skin. I would put on my mother's blouse. I also would put on her undergarments or bathing suit. I longed for a hug, a touch, feelings of acceptance. I leapt at the physical feeling as something to go back to at times when I felt bad.

It was when I was an early teenager, about 13 or so, that I began cross-dressing. It lasted at that time for about three or four years until I was 15 or 16, and I put it away. Later, around age 20 when my first marriage was on the rocks and my wife was terminally ill, I returned to it. I reviewed a movie for the newspaper on transvestites—I never knew that that existed, except of course by my earlier experience. I began completely cross-dressing at that time. I didn't feel very good about myself at all. I used cross-dressing as a way to feel good.

Therapist: How did you experience your body?

Patient: I didn't experience my body at all. I was at war with my body. I felt ugly, hairy, not muscular, and I got into trouble about masturbation. (I told my mother about it.) I didn't feel at home in my own body. If I could have changed it then I would have. I wanted to be more athletic, more muscular. I only weighed 140 when I got out of college. I had had nontropical sprue Celiac Syndrome—a malabsorption syndrome—from early on. I almost died of it at age 1 1/2. *When I put on my mother's clothes it was as if I had my mother's body.* I viewed women as a desirable thing to be.

Therapist: When you took off undergarments and would be reconfronted with your own male body, what did you experience?

Patient: I never wanted to be rid of my genitalia. It wasn't exciting, it didn't relieve anxiety. It was visual excitement. I could alter my appearance and produce a true feminine picture. It was self-exciting. When I was 23 to 30, when I was actually cross-dressing, masturbation was real good. Cross-dressing improved masturbation.

Therapist: What was your fantasy and what did you do?

Patient: I'd have a feeling like wanting a cigarette. My skin would tingle; I would be nervous. Then I would begin to plot time I'd have to myself when I could be free to cross-dress. I'd look forward with great anticipation: It may be a day, or two weeks from then, but I would plan and look forward to it. I'd acquire clothes and makeup. Then I would toss it away afterward, almost like a binge. It could also be like a binge and then I could go for months without it, and then it would be the most important thing in my life. The whole scenario would last two to three hours. I would do makeup, fingernails, all my clothes looking just right. Then I'd take polaroid shots so I could use them instead of cross-dressing later. I was looking for a sexually exciting female. I was looking for that to arouse myself.

Therapist: What was the most erotic? What, specifically, were you looking for?

Patient: Hair, lipstick, breasts, legs. *I'd appraise each surface of my body.* I'd sit in a chair or some mundane thing for about

15 minutes. Then I'd begin masturbation and draw it out as long as possible. I'd still look at the female aspects of myself as I masturbated.

Therapist: Were you responding to the figure in the mirror, or to another picture inside you, or to your own body?

Patient: I was responding to the figure in the mirror. I collected individual images and feelings and examined them carefully and put them away in my mind so I could call them up later (e.g., the tightness of a bra strap on my body).

Therapist: Was it a way to experience your body as real?

Patient: I don't know. I have never been attuned to my body. It had never seemed important. I guess it was a way I could feel more whole, and really feel my body—all of me. At those times, it didn't seem like there was a hole inside—like something was missing.

Therapist: Do you have a picture of your body in your mind?

Patient: I can't see myself. I can see myself as other people see me, but when I try, I'm not there. I have to get a picture of myself sitting in my office to have a picture of me. I saw a videotape of myself last week at a press conference. I saw a middle-aged, good-looking man. For the last few months, I've been concerned about this body I'm living inside of. I'd like to get to know it. I've used and abused it. It occurs to me that I'd better take care of it. At the press conference I wasn't seeing me, I was seeing what various people wanted of me.

Therapist: It sounds like a transition time for you: from living through others and their view of you, to being inside your own body and having your own reference point inside.

Patient: Yes, it's a stock-taking. And I think you may have been right about what you said earlier that something may have crystallized in my mind about turning 40 as being a time of stock-taking. I'm more than half-way through— where have I been and where am I going, and what will I take with me? When I remarried, at age 30, I put all the cross-dressing in the closet and locked it away. I would still use memories of it, and occasionally a magazine as stimulation to make myself feel OK. With increased

> stress and the need to perform for others, I used mastur-
> bation as a way to get *a hold on myself.* It was me, it was
> continuous. I was giving myself away in bits and pieces.

Therapist: It sounds like masturbation was one of the few things
              that you did just for yourself.

Patient: That's right. Probably the only one. I was just inside me
            then, not looking at me the way I thought others would
            see me, and living my life for others—for their approval.

Exhibitionism

Exhibitionism can be viewed as a primitive means of affirming
body intactness. The individual extracts a mirroring affirmation from
an audience in order to revitalize a depleted, failing sense of self (5).

The mirroring presence of a real or imagined audience is a crucial
element of many exhibitionistic fantasies and acts. The exhibitionistic
act is usually set in motion by a ruptured empathic bond of a specific
nature: the failed empathy (or overt humiliation) involves some perceived essential aspect of sexual worth. The repair of this experienced injury is to seek a "replacement selfobject"—an audience—
who can assure him of bodily and masculine intactness. The aston-
ished look is a response that the exhibitionist has effectively created,
affirming that his body and masculine equipment are not ignored. A
very similar psychodynamic and developmental profile was present
in a man whose treatment I supervised who was a compulsive
obscene telephone caller (for many, many years). His "exhibitionism"
was via the vivid pictures of himself he painted verbally.

Masochism

Some forms of masochism may arise from a basic desire to have an
impact on someone else. A masochist, for example, may want to
force expressions of love, of approval, and sympathy; to invoke guilt
and remorse; to provoke another; to inflict a symbolic beating. These
desires to affect another, to elicit responses, are a version of the basic
urge for mastery—to feel effective. One intent of each increment of
effectance and mastery is self-cohesion.

Joseph (6) reports that some masochistic patients enact their beating fantasies in front of a mirror, thus functioning as their own self-validating audiences. The outline of the body/self representation through real or imagined pain can be articulated by the symbolic "beatings" or pain of masochistic characters or moral masochists (1).

"Skin eroticism" is a frequently found feature in masochistic characters. There exists an excessive, predominant focus on skin stimulation and erotic forms of skin warming that outline a precarious body image. It has been postulated that the masochistic individual is specifically anxious about body intactness, because he has failed to consolidate a stable and integrated body image (7).

For an individual without a distinct body image or with a regressive fragmentation of the self, pain can be a means of creating a feeling of aliveness and realness. The receipt of pain establishes or reestablishes a boundary—an experience of existing as a bounded, contained entity.

> An adolescent girl repeatedly rubbed the skin on her arms with a pencil eraser until she bled in response to feelings that she was abandoned or did not exist. Prior to hurting herself, she would attempt various maneuvers to get her parents to respond to her; when they did not, she felt as if she didn't exist. She wanted to feel "real," and tried to establish real sensations through pain (and, unconsciously, the boundaries of her skin), validated by blood, confirmed later by scarring (a hypertrophied boundary). She was further reassured when she found that she could not erase herself. She was indelible, permanent. The pain, as well as her primitive sense of permanence, relieved her anxiety. The reality of her most basic self—her body—buttressed her feelings of realness, of existence. Self boundaries were restored, outlined by pain and accentuated by scars.
>
> Another young woman described scrubbing herself so hard with a brush at bathtime that her skin would be raw and bleeding. She indicated that this actually did not cause pain, but was relieving, reassuring to do. Her "scrubbings" began at pubescence, when she felt "dirty," and needed to "scrub away the dirtiness." She recognized, in reconstructions, that illnesses and accidents were the only way to effectively engage the concern and attention of her highly self-absorbed and largely absent mother. Earlier physical and sexual abuse had skewed the experience of her body and of pain, adding to an already-elevated pain threshold because of empathic neglect of sensorimotor development.

Some hypochondriacal symptoms represent an attempt to focus self-stabilization—a final regressive end point (the body)—in the quest for affirmation. As regressive fragmentation occurs, an individual becomes preoccupied with body function or parts in a concrete though unconscious effort at self restitution (1).

Mahler believes that a rudimentary body image is achieved through the stimulations of the child's body surface by the mother (8). Winnicott indicated that consistent, sensual holding and handling of the infant promotes the child's experience of himself as a unit, existing within his body, bounded by his skin (9).

Homosexuality

Homosexuality may represent active effort to repair developmental arrest by creating a sexualized self-selfobject bond. The following is an excerpt from a therapy interview with a 20-year-old man who demonstrates this principle.

Patient: Yesterday I saw a good-looking girl who smiled at me by the pool. I felt great. When I feel good about myself, I feel good physically about my body. I begin to not feel good about myself if someone insults my looks, or laughs at me, or if I do something stupid. When I feel bad about myself I feel anxious sexually. If I feel I'm going to be rejected (by peers or girls) then I'd feel like there's something wrong with me, a vague, uncomfortable, restless feeling. It's like I want something, but don't know what it is. Then I begin to focus on homosexual thoughts. Gay guys give you compliments; girls just treated me like I was ordinary. It was like I created my own world to deal with my anxiety—going to gay groups—and they were always eager and excited about me. The next morning, I would look in the mirror and said, "Hey, I used to know you." I wanted to climb into the mirror and come back inside myself—my friend. It reassures me that I'm liked and that I was worth something when guys would respond to me—to my body.

This vignette describes a typical scenario for this young man, initiated by a disruption in a selfobject bond and his resultant experience as an assault of self-esteem focused on body image. (The specific precipitant in this instance was a disruption in the narcissistic transference due to the therapist's vacation.) His restitutive attempt involved seeking an idealized male who would want him and find him attractive—who would not abandon him. The middle sequence, the symptom act, involves the patient's sexualizing an archaic, narcissistic configuration in an effort to find an eroticized replacement for a selfobject who was disappointing, absent, or unresponsive. The final sequence is the reestablishment of that bond with the important selfobject—or in a symptom scenario, the symbolic replacement of that selfobject or admiring and affected male.

Many sexual activities and perversions can represent attempts to counterbalance experiences of depletion or fragmentation. The sexual activity centers intense awareness of the body self, as well as the distinctness, separateness, and sensual response of two bodies.

THE BODY SELF IN THE OEDIPAL PHASE

The following two vignettes are from the psychoanalysis of a 31-year-old unmarried professional. His primary goal of analysis was to be able to have an intimate, committed relationship with a woman, which so far had eluded him. The first vignette is from a very early middle phase of analysis; the second from a late middle phase.

Vignette 1: Early Middle Phase

R. M. was examining his repeated patterns of becoming quickly and intensely involved with many women, yet with disappointment recognizing their "flaws" after a period of courtship. With an initial idealization of the woman, he would "lose" himself in them and their interests, giving himself entirely over to their pleasure and wishes, only to become disappointed and angry that he did not get nearly as much in return.

He described, upon meeting a desirable woman, feeling a sexual urge and desire for conquest. He came to recognize a component of this desire as wanting to enter a woman sexually and to emerge intact. At another level, he effected a fusion and blending (via body sexual parts) analogous to the emotional fusion and blending with his mother. He hoped unconsciously to emerge from the blending a separate and autonomous individual.

As a child he felt unable to say no to his narcissistic, socialite mother. If he refused to act in compliance with her wishes that she be the center of his life, she would withdraw in a depressive posture. R. M. would then feel alone and abandoned, as his father was absorbed in his own work and prominence. The mother was as emotionally hungry as she was beautiful, and R. M. felt that he was the only one who could console her at times of her protracted crying, and was the only person in the family who had the power to soothe her. This resulted in a peculiar blend of a sense of power and highly developed empathic skills to give women narcissistic gratification, yet a pervasive ineffectiveness to really change anyone or himself.

His desire to reenact a merger and emerge whole and intact (emotionally and via intercourse) was his repeated effort to establish the fusion and emerge separate (emotionally) and intact (physically and self).

He recognized that a protection from this fusion when he was especially feeling anxious was to have impotence so that he could not fuse physically. His physical impotence was viewed as a protection from this merger when his anxiety was especially high. He called this his "social impotence," which countered his not being able to set limits on what he wanted or needed when intensely involved with a woman. He felt highly embarrassed and helpless when impotence occurred.

Vignette 2: Late Middle Phase

Several months later in analysis, R. M. indicated that his penis was particularly small. When I asked for details, he seemed unable to be objective. I then asked him, "When was the last time you measured?" At first, laughing, he thought I was joking. When I assured him I was not, he responded, "Well, that's an interesting question. I don't know—I guess it was in early adolescence."

His associative material was then of comparing himself to his father in many ways. I suggested that perhaps his image of his body and penis vis-a-vis his father's was still the body image and comparison which he had in his mind: of his father being large, powerful, and himself being extremely small. He readily remembered an image when he was about five years old, as he recognized that he was very small, looking at a man who was very large, which remained as an active image in his mind; this image of himself, and of his penis in particular, had been retained from that earlier time. The angle of viewing of his father (looking upward), as well as his idealization, made both the image and the experience larger than life. His response which followed this recognition:

It just dawned on me that in the same way I have a distorted view of my penis, that maybe I view my body in the same distorted way. I always make sure I don't get in really great shape. I get almost there and then do things to stop and to counter my conditioning. I can get almost there but then something happens, and I stop. I've been afraid of getting fat, and I focus on my waist when I think about that. Its been almost two years that I've been seeing you and I've never had any idea that I'd be talking to you about this.

The vignette occurred in the midst of a highly charged transference neurosis in which he compared himself numerous ways, actual and fantasied, with the analyst to see if he "measured up." During this time, when experiencing impotence he felt there was something I could do or say that I was just withholding, which would keep him potent. His angry perception that I was "taking away his erection" paralleled the activation of a memory of having a urological operation at age five with his physician-father present. Dream and associative material confirmed his attribution of punishment because of his father's recognition of his too-intense involvement with his mother, and his total repression of this actual surgical event crystallizing castration anxiety by the actual physical trauma of bodily invasion.

REFERENCES

1. Stolorow, R., & Lachman, R. *Psychoanalysis of developmental arrests.* New York: International Universities Press, 1980.

2. Freud, S. *Fetishism.* (Standard ed., Vol. 21, pp. 175–194). London: Hogarth Press, 1964.

3. Person, E. The omni-available woman and lesbian sex: Two fantasy themes and their relationship to the male developmental experience. Unpublished paper.

4. Glasser, M. Identification and its vicissitudes as observed in the perversions. *International Journal of Psycho-Analysis, 67:* 9–31, 1986.

5. Kohut, H. *The analysis of the self.* New York: International Universities Press, 1971.

6. Joseph, E. (Ed.), Beating fantasies (Kris Study Group, Monograph I). New York: International Universities Press, 1965.

7. Keiser, S. The fear of sexual passivity in the masochist. *International Journal of Psycho-Analysis, 30:* 162–171, 1949.

8. Mahler, M., Pine, F., & Bergman, A. *The psychological birth of the human infant.* New York: Basic Books, 1975.

9. Winnicott, D. *The maturational process and the facilitating environment.* New York: International Universities Press, 1965.

5

Body Self and Psychological Self Integration Through Adolescence

In terms of object relation theory, selfobject functioning progresses developmentally from a merged entity to transitional, or intermediate, space between self and object to, finally, autonomous functioning with an internalized object. This sequence, in self psychological terms, represents the maturation of self-selfobject relationships.

We have learned that conflicts concerning autonomy and separateness recur throughout the individual's development and throughout each stage in the life cycle (1). Kohut (2) has taught us that adults continue to need mirroring self-affirmations, in maturing forms, throughout life. Modell (3) emphasizes the persistent need for transitional objects in mature love relationships, the

> illusion that one's safety in the world is assured by one's maintaining contiguity with a protective object. Even in a mature love relationship where the separateness of the loved object is fully affirmed, in another part of the mind that loved one will-function as a transitional object.

This process is paralleled in the body self experience as well as in the affect-experiencing psychological self experiencing affect. The primary caregiver functions as selfobject in affirming and organizing; accuracy and thoroughness of response to the body self and psychological self experience of the child allow identification and verbal affirmation of somatic states.

The early experience of deriving comfort and pleasure from one's body aids in establishing this as an ongoing process of desomaticizing, differentiating, and verbally mastering affect. Failure of this basic pleasure may lead to continued efforts to regulate affect by some external source, such as food or alcohol, or to neglect of one's body altogether in focusing on intellectual pursuits.

Human development is neither orderly nor linear. Natural times of enhanced awareness of the distinctness/integration of the body self and psychological self awareness occur at an initial separation-individuation with movement into early oedipal phase and again at pubescence (4).

The patients we have studied in the Eating Disorders Program have showed evidence of significant developmental arrest underlying their anorexia nervosa, bulimia, or compulsive eating disorder (5–8). This arrest affects most profoundly the narcissistic and separation-individuation process. Failure to negotiate cohesiveness in sense of self delays completion of separation; when such an individual faces the adolescent task of a changing body in the progress from pre-pubescent childhood to sexual young adulthood, symptoms erupt. One constellation of symptoms focuses on remaining thin, losing weight, or in some way delaying recognition of the body as pubescent, maturing, sexual. Such a person's body image, if formed, is asexual and prepubescent, even if the individual is well into adulthood (5). An understanding of developmental arrest and resulting pathological manifestations demonstrates the history of such a patient's relationship to his or her body. Girls and women with eating disorders have either not reorganized body changes or have denied the reality of the changes taking place. Thus, their body and their body images are different. Some individuals physically assault their bodies with compulsive exercise or actual traumatic abuse. Others engage in compulsive or impulsive actions that stimulate or excite the body, or in sexual activity, dangerous situations, or drugs.

The biological events of pubescence and a maturing physical and sexual body must be seen as a reality of the body self, as well as a metaphor for the evolving psychological self. In pathological development, the ongoing split (nonintegration) between mind and body will be in sharper focus because of the major increment of sexual development in early adolescence and will perhaps crystallize into overt symptoms for some.

TRANSITIONAL OBJECTS AND TRANSITIONAL RELATEDNESS

Winnicott (9) has demonstrated the developmental importance of solacing objects, including transitional objects. The comforting experiences, if they occur consistently and adequately, are internalized gradually so that the experience becomes an internal function. When the comforting internalization is incomplete, the person continues to seek and, to a limited degree, experience solace but fails to develop an independence from the external source (9). An attempt to create a transitional object may itself become a symptom if the object is a substance (disguised to soothe) such as alcohol, food, or drugs. A true transitional object is one that symbolizes a healthy relationship with the primary nurturing figure.

The choice of and relationship to transitional objects is highly idiosyncratic. The voice of the mother, coactional vocalization by the mother-infant dyad, and words or sounds by the individual are all examples of auditory-solacing experiences (9) which usually undergo transformation beyond early childhood.

The experience of internal solace and the ability to develop nurturing relationships represent a lifelong developmental process. Horton and Sharp (10) argue compellingly that maternal soothing, subsequent ego function, and solacing linguistic competence are all related. Infants reared without consistent, reliable comforting do not develop transitional object attachments (11) and often exhibit significant language deficits (12). An adult with alexithymia (difficulty with both the experience and language of emotion) (12) is exhibiting the developmental consequences of a lack of reliable solacing (10) and is predisposed to psychosomatic conditions.

THE BODY AS REALITY AND AS METAPHOR

Recognition of the importance of body experience in childhood provides an important key to understanding the way in which bodily experience and feelings play a prominent role not only in cognitive development but also in the development of the ability to think abstractly and symbolically. The physiologic mastery of body orifices develops in a parallel manner. Concurrent with the establishment of urethral and anal sphincter control, the child acquires language. The child becomes increasingly able to use speech to relieve the tension once dominated by physical discharge. Words substitute for bodily substances and experiences and provide the child a means for discharging ideas and expressing feelings.

The associative connection to bodily experiences in which sensation and affect are closely related can serve as an organizing principle for the therapist's listening. Body experiences are a major source of metaphoric thought and speech (13). A therapist has only to listen to the body-derived experiences in the associative material from a single patient's therapy session to recognize how basic they are to the core of cognitive-affective life. The fracture of connection between mind and body must be examined for developmental arrest versus conflict, or both. Revealing and affective, language is as predetermined as a slip of the tongue as emotional experiences find appropriate verbal imagery (10). Metaphor becomes personal, dynamically and emotionally significant. Verbal imagery corresponds to ideas and emotions, whether they are overt, repressed, or unconscious.

Metaphor describes the immediate self-state and often reveals physical state and bodily perception as well as the emotional experience of the moment ("I feel shut down"; "tight"; "it's like all the doors in my mind just closed"; "I feel calm all over when we talk in this way"; "I feel like I'm falling"; "I feel all disconnected inside"). There is often a direct mind-body connection ("My stomach just tightened up"; "I want to be pulled out of this depression"; "It's a dead feeling"; "I feel very heavy"). Some psychological states, especially depression, are experienced primarily as bodily states.

Case Vignette 1

The patient, a professional woman in her middle thirties, described feelings of aloneness and a yearning for intimacy. She recognized her desire to feel free and close to me in therapy, but was afraid she would not want to leave treatment if that were the case. I asked her to describe her experience, including her fantasies, in more detail.

Patient: I'm afraid I wouldn't be able to lift my body off the couch. What would you do if I couldn't leave?

Therapist: I hear your desire to stay and your fear of letting go at the same time.

Patient: I feel the full weight of my body on the couch now. It really feels different.

Therapist: You must be focusing inside yourself to be aware of all of your body.

Patient: Yes, it really feels different—like all of me is here. (Pause) I feel hungry.

Therapist: Physically or emotionally?

Patient: Both.

Therapist: Do you know the difference?

Patient: No. (Pause) When it's physical, it's in my stomach. I have probably taken more aspirin in the last two months than ever before. I've really been feeling tense.

Therapist: It's as if all the pain gets localized in your head.

Patient: I have always concentrated on my head—on my thinking and on my intellect rather than on my body. It really feels different to think about and experience my body, and to begin to put the two together.

Sharpe (14) has postulated that metaphor evolves concurrent with control of body orifices. As part of this postulate, the emotions originally accompanying bodily discharge find substitute channels and expression via metaphor. Spontaneous metaphor, when examined analytically, is a condensation of a forgotten experience and can reveal the psychophysical origin of a present psychic experience. Metaphor provides information about instinctual tension.

Metaphorical references to sexual encounters are often so explicit that they are comical, a "touch and go" relationship for the adolescent; the man who says, "Being with her is a series of ups and downs."

Individuals who have been subjected to the greatest amount of parental intrusiveness and control (exemplified in anorexics), harbor great fear of losing bodily control during stress. It has been demonstrated that eating disorder patients have a sense of estrangement from their bodies, insensitivity to body sensations, and blurred body boundaries (15).

Case Vignette 2

A young anorexic woman was describing the confusion and dissonance she experienced about her body. She described it in the following way:

The image I want to get to is normal and healthy, but I feel like a watermelon with toothpicks—really big. Yet I know in my head I need to gain weight. It doesn't make sense. It doesn't fit together—to gain weight when I feel big, and at the same time feeling that getting to normal would be to lose weight.

And further:

I feel like a little child. Anything more than a little child, like my body being big, feels really fat. Anything other than being a little girl when I feel that way, like having an adult body, makes me feel big, fat, too much.

This incongruous feeling was precipitated when the patient experienced adultlike, intimate feelings, and when an empathic bond with an important person was disrupted. Particularly good, connected-with-another feelings elicited anxiety because of the newness of the experience, which represented a significant departure from her model of herself as a little, ineffective, dependent, prepubescent girl.

Body and Psyche Changes in Adolescence

A girl of 16 related the onset of her bulimia to her recognition at 13 years of age that her parents had their own problems and struggles apart from her that were not her fault, as she had assumed previously. With the withdrawal of her parents into their own struggles, this already depleted young girl developed a thinly veiled abandonment depression.

Already on the brink of symptomatic difficulty with her new pubescent urges, body changes, and increased social pressure in school, her loss of connectedness with her parents precipitated an attempt to create a soothing "transitional object," food. As she ate, she could magically construct her parents in her mind and control their presence and giving of the nurturing object. By thrusting her behavior into her parents' awareness, she was able to elicit predictable (though negative) responses, which ensured their engagement and presence.

The patient's objectification and deidealization of her parents was a disillusioning confrontation of her separateness. Her fragile self-organization disintegrated, and she became actively bulimic in an attempt to adapt to a traumatic loss.

When asked to draw her body, the patient divided the page in half with a vertical line. On the left side, she drew a proportionate, distinct, cohesive body image, complete, yet undifferentiated and asexual. On the right side was a grotesquely overweight, disproportionate body that had protrusions in the stomach and leg areas. She explained that the normal-appearing image was how she looked when she felt good and things were going well for her. The image on the right represented her feelings and her image of herself when she felt bad, was depressed, rebuffed by others, or out of tune with things around her.

We examined in detail her experience of these body images. When she felt good, the drawing with the accurate boundaries corresponded to the image she saw when she looked in the mirror. However, when she felt bad, she saw herself as obese and said that that image corresponded exactly to what she saw in the mirror. She did not seem puzzled that at two different times she could see two entirely different figures in the mirror. When I asked her what she looked at *specifically* in the mirror, she indicated that when she felt good, she looked at her entire body, and when she felt bad and felt fat, she looked at the inner part of her thighs and occasionally at her stomach. She saw her inner thighs and hips as rounded, concluding that they were fat and that she was fat all over.

When we have asked other patients to describe the times when they feel fat, exactly what they mean by fat, where they experience the fatness, and what areas they look at in the mirror that validates their feelings of fatness, they have almost all confirmed the experience of the patient described above; the feeling of being fat stems from discordant emotional experience and is validated by a particular perception of a body part. Concluding the whole from a (perceived) part represents the logic of primary process and is a cognitive component of emotionally precipitated regression.

EMOTIONAL LANGUAGE

Developmental Deficits of Cognition and Language

Freud described two patterns of thinking, primary and secondary process (16). Primary process thinking arises from the desire to satisfy urges and drives, and the resulting representations are not bound by logic. Characterized by logic, temporal and spatial concepts, and verbal representations, secondary process encompasses conscious and preconscious thinking.

Extrapolation by others has defined in greater detail additional and more complex thinking patterns. The need to expand Freud's simplistic view is apparent when we see clinically that some individuals cannot understand feelings and still others cannot express them. Some patients find metaphors and symbolic representations, particularly those having to do with feelings, the self, and self experience, difficult to understand; this thinking does not fit into secondary process as Freud described it.

An example is the psychosomatic patient's inability to express feelings and understand expressions of feelings. Sifneos attributes this alexithymia to damage of the central nervous system through genetic error, infection, or organic injuries, including trauma (12). Others believe that the inability to develop concepts of experiences and feelings is a result of early childhood psychological or physical trauma (17).

Since patterns of thinking have their own developmental progression, they are subject to their own developmental arrest. In patients with narcissistic disorders, particularly involving psychosomatic disturbances, the cognitive arrest is at the level of operational thinking, with nonintegration and nondevelopment of patterns of thinking relating to the body self and psychological self; in other ways, the intellect relating and thinking of such individuals can be very highly developed. Such a patient may attempt to use deductive logic in explaining, for example, that he must have been sad or depressed because he cried.

Piaget considers sensorimotor concept formation to be the child's first mode of thinking (18). In this pattern of thinking, a child compiles sensory impressions and motor and spatial experiences, along with emotions. Termed emotional sensorimotor thinking, these experiences are present from the first months of life (19). When arrest occurs, they do not integrate with later patterns of thinking, memory formation, and emotional experience. Winnicott believes that these memories, composed mainly of sensory experiences that include visual, auditory, olfactory, and taste sensations, are physical experiences that are recreated (remembered) during analytic sessions via body experiences (9). (See next chapter.) He describes patients' having, during sessions or at home, sensory memories in which the body is felt to be altering shape or being moved around, and in which reactions from body organs are experienced, such as heart palpitations or breathing difficulty.

The organization of emotional sensorimotor thinking is primitive and fragmented, lacking in developmental integration. In calm states, it may be experienced only as a nonawareness of emotional or bodily experience, a nonintegration of mind and body. At more emotionally charged times, such as the disruption of an empathic bond, this form of thinking becomes more chaotic and is experienced as anxiety of disorganization. The experience of overwhelming dysphoria and helplessness may be organized at a somatic level; the individual attempts to return to his most basic foundation of experience, his body, and stimulate it to create an organizing emotional focus. Food, exercise, drugs, or other physical stimuli are the usual means by which this organization is accomplished, the result being somatic attunement and partial reorganization.

A young bulimic woman states this dynamic succinctly:

> When I feel unfocused, I have no image of myself. I get really scared. It's like looking in the mirror and seeing no image. I ask myself "Do I exist? Where am I? Who am I?" As long as I overeat, I have a miserable, heavy stomach. That's *something*, though.

Both operational thinking and emotional sensorimotor thinking are relied on by developmentally arrested individuals as they attempt to reorganize and reintegrate at times of overwhelming affect. Secondary process thinking is a developmentally advanced integration of primary process thinking, operational thinking, and emotional sensorimotor thinking (19). Secondary process thinking appears during the second year of life as the more primitive thinking patterns are integrated. It accelerates remarkably with the formal use of symbol formation and normal verbal development.

With failure of development of cohesive body and psychological self, an intense self-absorption manifests, making self-reflection and self-observations difficult for these individuals. They remain, as Piaget (18) stated, "immersed in personal images and inexpressible feelings." This mode of thinking is characteristic of earlier development and attests to cognitive and emotional developmental arrest. Components of this cognitive developmental arrest include magical thinking, the "all or nothing" experience of emotion, and the assumption that others are an extension of one's self, automatically understanding and sharing one's thoughts and feelings without their being verbalized. An individual developmentally arrested at the cognitive level is unable to consider an alternative to his view that the part represents the whole, that a component of self, body, person, or event is, indeed, the whole thing; he is not able to consider several components of something and integrate them. The anorexic is an example. She looks at herself in the mirror, and focuses on one part of her anatomy (such as stomach or the curve of the inner thighs), concluding when she sees some curvature that she is fat all over.

In an extensive study, Weisberg et al. (20) found the most distinctive characteristic of bulimics to be their self-preoccupation and self-investment. They discovered in these individuals a disturbance in self-experience and deficits in self-esteem regulation together with precarious and fragile self-organization. Goodsitt (21) found, as we have (5), that the symptomatology of eating disorders is related to a desperate attempt to restore and preserve a malformed sense of self.

An individual feeling helpless and out of control seeks control over his own body. Many patients have described becoming more aware of their bodies, rather than less, when they exert ultimate control, which may come from food, compulsive exercise, or the use of laxatives or diuretics.

The eating-disordered patient may, at times, focus exclusively on thighs, buttocks, and stomach. The ultimate intent of this body hyperawareness and vigilance is the maintenance of a sense of control and effectiveness. "My stomach is my life—my focus. It affects how I feel"; "I'm aware of what I look like to others—I want to be picture-perfect."

Exercise provides the experience of repetition, of predictability, of being in control of what will happen next. Feeling effective is even more important to these individuals than feeling good physically. Tight and distinct muscles afford a specific body awareness and proprioceptive and kinesthetic feedback.

THERAPEUTIC IMPLICATIONS

The most basic arrests in the developmental synthesis of body and psyche manifest in psychosomatic disorders, which include eating disorders. Emotions do not extend beyond bodily expression; they do not become desomatized when this developmental integration is stalled. The essence of psychosomatic symptomatology is the return to an archaic, preverbal mode of expression and interaction. The purpose of these symptoms ultimately is attunement in some way to the body self when estrangement has occurred and acquisition of needed responses from selfobjects.

The function of the therapist (the current selfobject) is to accurately recognize and assist in articulating affective states. Affect evolves from somatic experience to differentiation of types of affect to verbalization about them. The empathic therapist facilitates this progression.

Verbalization not only provides mastery by articulating feelings, but also, more importantly, it facilitates the integration of body self and psychological self. The blending of affective and cognitive, bodily and psychic self, consolidate a sense of self.

Because of the cognitive and emotional developmental arrests, which include magical thinking, all-or-nothing perception, the desire for immediate response or result, and an intolerance for anxiety and ambiguity, it is difficult for the narcissistic patient, particularly the narcissistic action-oriented adolescent, to recognize the benefits of psychotherapy. The wish for immediate results makes such an individual prematurely judge the value and effectiveness of therapeutic intervention; the desire for immediate relief is concrete, externally oriented, and initially not amenable to an introspective approach. Alcohol, drugs, food, sexual encounters, and narcissistically based relationships all provide immediate, though only temporary, gratification.

The desire for a more permanent solution and the wish to engage meaningfully with the therapist as with other people is experienced as unsafe, possibly threatening, because of the patient's assumption that such a relationship would be as unreliable as past experiences have been. The desire to be effective and to impose predictability is a major factor that may have to be addressed early in the therapeutic encounter.

A patient may be quite invested in his symptomatology, since symptoms powerfully affect self-experience and assist in the preservation of narcissistic equilibrium, despite the distress they may manifestly cause. It is difficult and anxiety-provoking for a patient to consider relinquishing the power his symptoms confer—bingeing to achieve calm or purging for relief—and the incorporation of the symptom into his identity.

Such symptoms often cannot be abandoned in order to get better, but may diminish in intensity and utility over time in therapy. Consistent attention and therapeutic integration by both therapist and patient must be accorded the status and use of the symptoms.

REFERENCES

1. Modell, A. *Object love and reality.* New York: International Universities Press, 1968.
2. Kohut, H. *The analysis of the self.* New York: International Universities Press, 1971.
3. Modell, A. Self-preservation and the preservation of the self. *Annual of Psychoanalysis, 12, 13:*69–86, 1984–1985.
4. Laufer, M. The female Oedipus complex and the relationship to the body. *Psychoanalytic Study of the Child, 41:*259–276, 1986.
5. Krueger, D., & Schofield, E. Dance-movement therapy with eating disorder patients. *Arts in Psychotherapy, 13:*323–331, 1987.
6. Krueger, D. The "parent loss" of empathic failures and the model symbolic restitution of eating disorders. In D. Dietrich, & P. Shabab, *The problems of loss and mourning: New psychoanalytic perspectives.* New York: International Universities Press, 1988.

7. Krueger, D. Body self, psychological self, and bulimia: Developmental and clinical consideration. In H. Schwartz (Ed.), *Bulimia: Psychoanalytic treatment and theory.* New York: International Universities Press, 1988.

8. Donatti, D., Thibodeaux, C., Krueger, D., & Strupp, K. Sensory integration of body image distortions in eating disorders patients. Unpublished paper.

9. Winnicott, D. Transitional objects and transitional phenomena. *International Journal of Psycho-Analysis, 34:*89–97, 1953.

10. Horton, P., & Sharp, S. Language, solace, and transitional relatedness. *Psychoanalytic Study of the Child, 39:*167–194, 1984.

11. Arkema, P. The borderline personality and transitional relatedness. *American Journal of Psychiatry, 138:*172–177, 1981.

12. Sifneos, P. The prevalence of "alexithymic" characteristics in psychosomatic patients. *Psychotherapy & Psychosomatics, 23* (1), 255–263, 1973.

13. Sharpe, E. *Collected papers on psychoanalysis.* London: Hogarth Press, 1950.

14. Sharpe, E. Psychophysical problems revealed in language: An examination of metaphor. *International Journal of Psycho-Analysis, 21:*201–213, 1940.

15. Stroker, M., Goldberg, I., Green, J., & Saxon, J. Body image disturbance in anorexia nervosa during the acute and recuperation period. *Psychological Medicine, 9:*695–701, 1979.

16. Freud, S. *Formulations on Two Principles of Mental Functioning* (Standard ed., Vol. 12). London: Hogarth Press, 1911.

17. Marty, P. *L'Ordre psychosomatique.* Paris: Payot, 1980.

18. Piaget, J. *Judgment and reasoning in the child.* Totowa: Littlefield, Adams, and Co., 1959.

19. Basch-Kahre, E. Patterns of thinking. *International Journal of Psycho-Analysis, 66:*455–470, 1985.

20. Weisberg, L., Norman, D., & Herzog, D. Personality functioning in bulimia. Unpublished study.

21. Goodsitt, A. Self regulatory disturbances in eating disorders. *International Journal of Eating Disorders, 2:*51–60, 1983.

6

Eating Disorders: A Model Developmental Arrest of Body Self and Psychological Self

The histories and current clinical findings of patients with anorexia nervosa and bulimia nervosa indicate that early preverbal developmental arrest results in a failure to develop a distinct and separate body self, body boundaries, and accurate body image (1, 2). Subsequent developmental difficulties include a failure to achieve a cohesive sense of self, pathological narcissism, and separation-individuation defects. Distorted or nonformed body image is a basic developmental deficit in people coming to treatment for eating disorders. This nonintegration (rather than defensive splitting) of mind and body is related directly to deficient self-regulation in eating disordered patients.

Effective treatment of these developmentally based illnesses is directed toward formation of cohesive physical and psychological selves and integration of early developmental issues not otherwise verbally accessible.

Individuals with anorexia nervosa and bulimia nervosa suffer from disorders of their sense of self, a form of pathological narcissism.

Their ability to meaningfully describe themselves and their feelings is limited in a way that reveals them as different from many other patients typically seen in psychiatric treatment. Like many other psychosomatic patients, they constrict emotional expression and tend to describe extraordinary details of symptoms as substitutes for feelings and internal experiences. They inhibit fantasy, limiting their capacity to symbolize and to play. They are often affluent, educated, and privileged, and the adults are usually in positions of responsibility and prestige requiring energy, intellect, and ability. Despite this, they are unaccustomed to accepting themselves as a point of reference, or of describing their own internal experience. They perform for others, are perfectionistic, and yearn for recognition (3). They engage in obsessive vigilance about their bodies, food, calories and how they appear to others.

Individuals with eating disorders enter treatment as less insightful, verbal, and psychologically minded regarding their own self-awareness than their intellectual level would indicate. They often know as much as the therapist about theory and psychodynamics, but have not been able to apply their knowledge to effect personal change. Many patients I see have had at least one course of therapy in the past, but they have been unable to use the insight and interpretations of meanings from traditional dynamic psychotherapy, and supportive therapy has been insufficient for their needs (3, 4).

Patients who suffer from anorexia nervosa and bulimia nervosa have an inadequate internal regulation system, to the extent that they may be unable to recognize such basic body sensations as hunger. They oscillate rapidly between grandiosity and self-depreciation, relying vulnerably on external cues. They may obsessively count calories or weigh themselves numerous times a day. They cannot accept themselves or even their bodies without obsessively repeated external validations.

PSYCHODYNAMIC ASPECTS

Particularly at times of major increments of separation-individuation, the body assumes a crucial importance. An emergence of sexuality occurs in pubescence; separation from the parental home in young adulthood necessitates independent functioning. At these major developmental junctures, as well as at such others as marriage and pregnancy, some individuals become aware of their pervasive reliance on external cues to direct them, and of the absence of an internal center of initiative and regulation.

At some of these nodal points, especially early pubescence and pregnancy, the body will actually feel different, look different, and function differently. Physical appearance becomes especially important at these times of social and emotional adjustment. Family issues, such as the parents' response to the emerging sexuality of the adolescent, or the husband's reaction to pregnancy, become prominent elements in how the individual processes the changes within her body. The body of the boy becoming more like that of his father and the girl more like that of her mother during adolescence solidifies identificatory processes, or fractures them if there is a conflictual need to disidentify.

Adolescence is typified by evolving cognitive as well as physical capacities, and the experience of exploring new physical and conceptual vistas. Formal operations generate advanced abstraction and symbolism. Transitional objects during this time become more abstract, more diverse, and more creative. Cars, clothing, and a personal living space replace the immediate body, thumb, blanket, or teddy bear.

In normal development, increasing separation, autonomy, and acceptance of bodily changes all enhance the integration of physical and psychological selves with the expanding experience of effectiveness and mastery.

Narcissistic individuals do not advance beyond the stage of using their bodies as their transitional objects (5). Their developmental arrest includes the arrest of the cognitive capacity to symbolize selfobjects without effective separation and individuation; self-selfobject distinction is blurred and incomplete. Disengagement and symbolization of the selfobject are incomplete. The affected individuals have not objectified and symbolized their bodies: their bodies are still used as transitional objects, and they have failed to progress beyond preoperational *symbolic equations* to such complex cognitive and object-relational capacities as *symbolism* of self, body, and other.

Maintenance and control of self-other boundaries is a lifelong process. In the narcissistic individual, the sense of the body remains a central focus, and can never be accepted and internalized as long as development is stalled at this level. The body as a transitional object fails to gradually lose meaning as it does (and as transitional objects do) in normal development.

The individual who has never completely integrated body self and psychological self has difficulty resolving an essential addiction to maternal part-objects. The excessive reliance on selfobjects supplements functioning. This continuing need is alternately gratified or denied in the arena of the body. Symbols of autonomous selfhood are either lacking or totally confined to the context of bodily experience. The developmental arrest affects body self and schema, psychological self, and some cognitive capacities, particularly those influencing the sense of one's self as a whole and the permanence and completeness of body image.

These disorders manifest as deficiencies of self-regulation. Food is used as an external replacement for a deficient internal regulator and a deficient integration of mind and body. Relying on other people for their supply of affirmation, enhancement, function, and esteem, they attempt to find a way to internalize the source of these emotional goods. The frenetic pace of excruciating exercise, running, and swimming characteristic of the anorexic may appear to be for the purpose of losing weight, but is actually a desperate attempt to experience the reality of their bodies, for which they do not have an accurate or distinct mental representation. It is also an effort (as is controlling eating, or of vomiting) at countering the anguish of internal emptiness, boredom, and deadness. As a young anorexic woman explained it, "I feel completely helpless and ineffective, and I don't know what's wrong or how to feel better. At least when I focus on food and feel fat, I have *something* I can control and do something about."

Many anorexics have experienced emotional deprivation imposed by others, and unconsciously choose to convert their role as passive victims to the role of active victim by imposing deprivation (of food) upon themselves. The anorexic establishes an artificial boundary by saying no to food proffered by parents. In a quest for her own identity, she creates a distinctness by her opposition to her parents and to her own hungry body. Her body is viewed as an unintegrated part of her environment, something that must also be resisted. Her food refusal is a demonstration of independence from her parents, an effort at mastery to focus concretely that which is otherwise incomprehensible. The result is a visible need for nurturance and care as her body becomes weaker and more childlike.

The bulimic patient attempts to supply for herself what is missing via the symbolic equation of food and nurturance. This dynamic, incorporating symbolism and magical thinking, was summarized by a patient who said, "It's like I have anything and everything I've always wanted when I am in the middle of a binge. And I don't even have to pay the price of getting fat by getting rid of it all immediately."

The anorexic, the bulimic, and some compulsive overeaters experience a dreaded state of feeling that their bodies, indeed their self-organization, is easily invaded, influenced, exploited, and overwhelmed by external focus (especially important people).

Individuals with eating disorders have little or no recognition of an internal center of initiative or reference (6). They have struggled for their entire lives to be perfect in the eyes of others, to please others, or to reconstitute themselves to gain some sense of recognition, identity, effectiveness, and control.

Clinical Sequence: A Vignette

The following case of Jennifer was chosen as representing the most typical symptom/dynamic composite. Jennifer, a college senior, had a four-year history of bulimia nervosa, worsening at the beginning of her senior year, two months prior to her presentation for treatment. As we examined in detail a bulimic episode, she described first being aware of a mixture of feeling empty and uncomfortable, sometimes depressed. She turned immediately to food, with a desire to numb the emptiness. During the binge itself, she felt pleasure, sometimes euphoria. She experienced a magical omnipotence in which she could have, for a moment, whatever she wanted, entirely within her control. During the binge itself she often was frantic, rushed, or anxious. After the binge, she experienced a distended and painful stomach. This gave her "bad" feeling both reality and localization; additionally it was something she created—both by the action sequenced of bingeing and by the "bad" food chosen: sweets or "junk" food. Her dysphoria was now an entity that had form, shape, and remedy. She could actively and immediately rid herself of the problem by purging. "Feeling fat" was deemed the cause of feeling bad. Various active maneuvers could then be directed at this malady: dieting, taking diuretics, giving enemas, taking laxatives, and, especially, incessant exercise. By taking one or more of these directives, she could achieve the illusion of control by controlling actions of her body; literally to get rid of what she had eaten (the bad feeling/object). Then followed a period of feeling guilty for doing one of these actions, interspersed with feeling tired and relieved at having managed these events. She tried desperately to control her overwhelming compulsion to exercise. She reported, "I tried and tried not to give in and exercise, but the anxiety was overwhelming. I felt that if I didn't exercise I would lose it—that I would just fade into everyone else around me. Then I'd be like everyone else—not special."

She regressively attempted to vividly reestablish her body self experience and boundaries—to feel real and distinct. Her stimulation and reintegration of her basic body self was, at the time, a primitive but effective effort at psychic reorganization.

A tenuous equilibrium was established until the next precipitant.

The precipitant, important to reconstruct in therapeutic work, was typically a disruption in a self-selfobject bond, with the impending or actual disconnectedness with an important person. A narcissistic hurt followed immediately, with the resultant emptiness or rage.

Feeling "bad" was the result for Jennifer of feeling ineffective: particularly ineffective in either maintaining an empathic connectedness with an important other, or in maintaining a connectedness with the ideal self (which was unattainable, as her goal was perfection). Her unattainable goals of perfection particularly centered on grades, weight, and other highly valued social referents.

Jennifer vividly described this process of attempting to find something external, concrete, and specific to be able to control, in order to feel effective when her internal state was unfocused. "When I felt empty and lonely as a girl, I would wish something really bad would happen to me, so then I would have a real reason for feeling really terrible, like an accident and bleeding, so others could see my hurting and believe it; then I could believe it too and know what it was. I didn't understand what was the matter. After I had something bad that would happen to me in my fantasy, then I'd feel better. When it's inside and no one sees it, you just want people to know, to be able to see it. Maybe then it would feel more real. I would also daydream about after I came to make something bad happen, then I would have someone to comfort me. I would imagine, for example being hit on the head and getting a bruise so that someone could see it, so they could see I was hurt. I would actually do that at times, but then I'd feel embarrassed and hide it even though I wanted someone to care for me and comfort me. Recently when I binge, and feel fat, and see my distended stomach—it is something for me to feel bad about. I created it. I wished to get skinny so that people could see how skinny I was and see me as sick. Sometimes I wish they'd find something wrong with me physically so they could see it and get rid of it."

The search for a focus for dysphoric affect is an attempted mastery, of converting passivity to activity, and an attempt to be effective in eliciting a specific response/validation from an important selfobject.

Jennifer recognized more detail. "I feel helpless, worthless that I can't control how someone responds to me. That's what brings me back to my body—to be destructive at least—to binge. It's a substitute for the things I can't get and want. I'm out of control. I take in something to feel better, then I feel more in control." As I commented that this must seem the only way at the moment that she can feel effective, she responded, "Yes. If it's not the way I want it to be, I can eat my way into feeling better—at least for a little while. Then I'm back to where I was before. Miserable."

I indicated that at least, though, she determined this misery. Her response: "Yes. I brought that about. At least I'm in control of something. It's also a substitute for the intimacy that I can't seem to achieve with anyone. It makes me feel better. It calms the anxiety. Bingeing and purging makes me feel slowed down and tired. It makes me blank out, and I don't have to think, and for that moment I don't have to think about how bad I feel."

She further indicated one bite could initiate her binge, thinking of it as "all or nothing." I interpreted how it was as if she were not responsible at that point. She agreed that she readily abdicated responsibility, then added that it was probably her wish to not grow up, to not assume full responsibility for what she did.

"What I do to feel good hasn't worked. Feeling good is going to have to come from someone else. It's more important what someone else thinks. If you think about yourself, you'll end up not having anything. I think, 'so what' of what I think. My opinion is worthless." I pointed out how her active process of invalidation, and of not listening to herself from inside, results in a feeling of worthlessness.

She felt ineffective at getting her parents to respond to her feeling and perceptions. Her conclusion, present from early childhood, was that she was not good enough, and needed to try harder. More achievement, more attractiveness, thinness, seemed to her to be the answer.

We reconstructed, from an adaptive context, the usefulness of her symptom. While the search had been for magical cure, her intent was to regulate her affect and sense of self during the pretreatment symptomatic time using food as the symbol of the nurturing selfobject.

BODY IMAGE PATHOLOGY AND EATING DISORDERS

The early developmental arrests that affect the sense of self seem to be based on the absence of a coherent, cohesive, organized body image. These individuals have a poor or absent sense of their body boundaries (6, 7, 8). Lacking internal evocative images of a body self or a psychological self, they rely on external feedback and referents, such as the reactions of others to their appearance and actions, or mirrors. There is a distinct lack of object and internal image constancy.

Sugarman and Karash postulate that an arrest occurs at the earliest stage of transitional object development, in which there is a failure to adequately separate physically and cognitively from the maternal object (5). This thesis is based in the tenet that the infant's body is the first transitional object on the path to separation and individuation.

Bruch first described the crucial role of the body image in eating disorders (3). The association between body image distortion, specifically overestimation of body image, and anxiety, depression, physical anhedonia, and a sense of pervasive ineffectiveness has been demonstrated by other investigators (8, 9). The severity of this body image distortion has been correlated with the poorest prognosis (10) and the highest and earliest relapse rate after treatment (7).

Psychoanalytic explanations of eating disorders have been based in a limited way on a psychosexual model. This model emphasizes a regression from phallic, oedipal issues to oral conflicts, and the bodily emaciation is viewed as a secondary retreat to a prepubertal condition. Bruch stressed interpersonal, familial, and ego disturbances (4). Only most recently has an object-relations model been proposed, in which patients with eating disorders are seen to have developmental difficulties in the separation-individuation process with disruptions and distortions of the underlying self and object representations (11).

Bruch (3) described the outstanding aspects of the anorexic as disturbances of body image and concept, defects in the accuracy, perception, and interpretation of stimuli from within the body, and a paralyzing and pervasive sense of ineffectiveness. The central feature of all three predominant symptoms is the experience, perception, and image *of the body*. Other clinicians traced the initial interruption to the state of separation-individuation (8, 9), crystallized during the third year of life.

These observations can be advanced to include the postulate that the failure to achieve autonomy and separation stems from an even earlier nucleus of arrested development, encountered when the nascent sense of self emerges from mirroring experiences with the mother in the first weeks and months of life. This process extends in changing forms throughout development. The preverbal experiences in the first year of life have failed to acknowledge and confirm a body self separate from the mother (1, 6, 12, 13). It is as if the mother is incapable of accurate, consistent mirroring, of reflecting the child's aliveness, special distinctness, and body and psychic boundaries. In such cases the mother is unable to allow the child the opportunity for an autonomous, internally directed origin of experience and action.

A component of the initial evaluation is a body image drawing. The patient is asked to draw (with crayon, for nonerasure) the picture she has in her mind of her body. Results from the study of these projective drawings and other evaluation measures of body image nondevelopment are detailed in chapter 3. The body images drawn by bulimics are blurred, indistinct and distorted; almost all indicate that the patient sees herself as much larger than she is. The body images drawn by anorexics are childlike and asexual, often have incomplete and permeable boundaries, and lack any distinguishing internal or external features.

These patients are not simply denying their body images, for they have never formed them. This is why the anorexic can never attain an ideal body weight and image: she doesn't have one. Thus she keeps trying to find the elusive answer. Nothing is ever enough because there is no end point—no internal ideal to achieve, and no internal model to use as orienting guidance. The developmental arrest has precluded the formation of a distinct ego ideal.

This indistinctness of body boundaries is equivalent to the blurring of emotional boundaries with another individual. Where one individual ends and another begins becomes a matter of emotional uncertainty.

Some very specific developmental functions have either not occurred or have occurred without sufficient completeness to provide a consistent nucleus for further evolution. Specifically, we have seen evidence that some preverbal and early verbal experiences forming the beginning body self have not developed (12), as though these children's emotions and their bodies were not seen by the parents as separate entities. The parents are typically unable or unwilling to perceive the child as an independent person with a distinct body, feelings, and initiative.

Winnicott (14) has speculated that the mother's face serves as a mirror for her baby. The sensitive mother is attuned to the feelings emanating from the infant and is able to reflect them in her expressions. The less-successful mother recognizes only her own feelings and not her baby's.

Sensorimotor events initiate the first self and object awareness and representations in the earliest developmental period (14). Awareness of the selfobject is in effect a very tentative distinction between the infant and his interactions. The selfobject at this point of development is thus almost entirely embedded within the infant's action sequence (5). The infant's body is his immediate experience of self through reflection, resonance, and internalization of the selfobject. One's body is the first object and tool of experience, the original substance which can be touched, smelled, and kinesthetically felt. The first external objects are the transitional items that evoke the illusion of the mother. The transitional object is simultaneously external and internal, a creation of the toddler representing both himself and mother. It further represents development away from reliance on the mother's physical presence, and the capacity to evoke a representation of her.

The ego and psychological sense of self emanate from this early body self (6). This seems to form the basis for an accurate representation of the self, individually fashioned. If the infant's sensations, movements, and affects are not regularly and accurately acknowledged and affirmed, or if they are supplanted by the mother's own needs, and *her* internal state is projected onto the baby, the baby's development of a sense of self will necessarily be affected. The process of affirmation continues in varying degrees throughout development. A false or distorted body image and the failure to recognize an internal focus of sensation is a basic element in the narcissistic pathology underlying most eating disorders. The nucleus of this pathological process occurs during the earliest formation of the sense of self, in the autistic and symbiotic stages of life before separation-individuation begins. The *preverbal experiences* in the first year of life typically have failed to acknowledge and confirm a *separate body self* from the mother for individuals who present during early adulthood with eating disorders.

These individuals' nuclear sense of self has not been cohesively formed, and remains disorganized and primitive. They have never integrated mind and body and are therefore unable to deny or defensively split them. The resulting maladaptive behaviors represent deficits rather than conflicts. The individual may not be simply denying a painful affect, she may have not developed an ability to recognize or distinguish different affects and bodily sensations. The narcissistic individual may not have a consolidated body image to either deny or achieve.

The developmental task is the formation of a stable, integrated, cohesive mental representation of one's body—a core body image of what is inside, what is outside, and a distinct sense of boundaries between the two. The creation of an individual internal space and the evolution of a psychological self typically occur simultaneously.

Disturbances in differentiating self and other affect the ability to create symbols, to distinguish the symbol from the object symbolized, and in turn promote an arrest at concrete thinking (15).

Lacking an ability to distinguish symbols from objects symbolized, the affected individual elicits a self-representation from her own body. The representation of self must emerge from the body self experience, not from a symbolic representation of the self, because, for these individuals, a viable representational image of the self has never developed. The psychological distance required for developmental progress beyond a transitional object is unavailable at this concrete, nonsymbolic operational level. *Symbolic equations* rather than *true symbols* predominate (16). Symbolic equations differ from true symbols because they are experienced as the actual object rather than as an emblem of it. With a symbolic equation, there is no "as if" quality. The individual must engage in body-oriented action or stimulation to regain the need-meeting object. Events that in some way stimulate the body (pain, gorging, starvation, overexertion) create a sensorimotor experience of the body self. Food is the vehicle used to achieve an experience of a self within the body and to recreate the feelings associated with the mother's presence.

Sugarman and Karash (5) assert that these individuals, because of their concrete, nonsymbolic mode of operation, are not able to move to an external nonbodily transitional object. They seem instead to struggle to create a transitional object that is external, concrete, and specific. This transitional object becomes food, and it is temporarily able to regulate affective states. The effectiveness of the object is fleeting, however, and can remain no more fixed in emotional consciousness than the defective internal images of body, self, or other.

Food is the first transitional object—the bridge between mother and infant. It is not the mother, but it represents her, and is an extension of her body. Food is, however, more a symbolic equation than a true symbol.

The psychological deficits I am describing here are most profoundly elaborated in the disorders of mind and body known as anorexia and bulimia. The pathological developmental course that leaves the young individual with a defective or absent body image, sense of wholeness, and impaired function is the preverbal bedrock of missed experience that appropriate therapeutic efforts must address.

THERAPEUTIC APPROACH

Empathic Immersion

The mother meets the infant's needs so unobtrusively that the infant does not experience his needs as needs. Initially, there are no symbols for this unity, because there is no distance to transcend with a symbol. Winnicott (15) proposes that the mother-infant unit must have *potential* space between the two that embodies a paradox: the mother and infant are one (in function) and the mother and infant are two (entities).

Only with the onset of frustration does the awareness of separateness begin, usually at about three-to-four months of age (17). The infant then recognizes that the mother is not an actual extension of his needs, wishes, and body, and he begins the long process of developing increasing mastery of his environment.

An equivalent potential space must exist between therapist and patient: one *function* and listening position occupied by two individuals.

The therapist must immerse himself in the patient's experience and psychic reality and respond in a way that communicates his understanding of them. Listening from within the patient's emotional consciousness and understanding her experience is the essence of the therapeutic empathy necessary to accurate interpretation and effective intervention.

The integration of approaches from different clinical positions within this developmental framework is organized around therapeutic empathy, listening from *within* the patient, rather than as an observer. The focus is on the internal experience of the patient's emotions, perceptions, ways of thinking, and causal explanations. Empathy becomes a bridge of understanding between patient and therapist—the echo in one of the voice in another. When this process is successful, patients can ultimately become empathic with themselves and regulate their own sense of self (18, 19).

Recognition of the Adaptive Context of Symptoms

In disorders of self-regulation, the individual seeks external regulators to supplement internal deficiencies. There is prominent reliance on other people for needed supplies of affirmation, enhancement, function, and esteem, and attempts to find a way to internalize these sources. There is outward conformity to the expectations of others, attempts to mold themselves to these expectations, and a parallel, often unconscious, urge to oppose others as a way of establishing boundaries and expressing destructive feelings.

There is nothing so frightening as a formless fear. Attaching form to the fear instills a kind of mastery and counters helplessness. Even if the form is not a causal fit, it may be compulsively evoked again and again to quell anxieties. The process of focusing control on food provides a concrete, external referent. Symbolic nurturance (bingeing) and self-imposed deprivation (anorexia) provide only transient relief from painful fears and feelings of discontrol.

Particularly in the initial phase of alliance formation with the patient, it is useful to view the patient's symptoms from an adaptive context, beginning on the surface, from her experience.

Vignette 1: 21-year-old Woman with Anorexia Nervosa

Patient:	My body grew up without me. I never got any affirmation that I liked myself. I shut myself off to try to focus on pleasing my parents. It was hard for me to see any good I do naturally. I had to have someone tell me what to do and became that. It's still difficult to form my own ideas. I feel very alone now when I'm self-sufficient and make my own decisions. It's frightening.
Therapist:	And it is confusing to yearn for and to fear the same thing.
Patient:	And especially to want oneness and connectedness, yet detest it too and want my separateness. When I didn't eat, everyone, my family, the other (previous) therapists, all wanted me to eat, and saw it as a problem—like a flaw or defect.
Therapist:	It must have been confusing and hurtful at a time when you were experiencing it as a particular accomplishment.
Patient:	The only real one in my life. But a destructive one.
Therapist:	Yet you described how your *intent* wasn't destructive, even if the *result* was.
Patient:	My intent was to be separate and to be my own person—to have control of my life. If you'd tried to force or control my eating when I came to you, it'd have been just like my parents. If you'd tried to reward me for eating, I wouldn't have found my own direction and motivation from inside me.

I realize how I've tried to be so perfect—to try to please others. I didn't even know myself. To feel connected to others I'd go along with anything they wanted—to go along with the crowd. I'd never do anything to be threatening or assertive.

Therapist: Yet you've also described how much you want to feel special, distinct.

Patient: Whenever I do, I feel criticized. Like my mother is telling me all the things I'm doing wrong or not good enough.

Therapist: It's as if your mother is always there—an image you're always creating.

Patient: She definitely haunts me. It's like I have to live up to her expectations 24 hours a day. I feel like I'm sneaking food even when no one is around. She's always there.

Therapist: For you to defy.

Patient: Yes.

Therapist: At least you're never alone that way.

Patient: Well, she's not physically present. It is her image in my mind. I see what you mean. It's hard to think about giving that up—it's been there for so long, like she's always with me. Telling me what to do. And I oppose so much of it. It takes a lot of energy.

Therapist: It must.

Patient: It sounds frightening at first to tell her goodbye and to create my own standards to live up to.

Without internal referents, the patient is inclined to compensate by focusing on something concrete and external that can be controlled—an explicit metaphor to emotionally replace what is missing internally. Food is experienced as the quintessential metaphor for the giving, loving, nurturing selfobject who has been lost or was never present.

The first words used are metaphors for the body, and its separateness from the mother. The infant who learns to say no states a distinctness from the parent. No says, "I am not an extension of you. I am me, and I am in charge of me." This is also the attempt of the anorexic who says no to food proffered by her parents: "I don't need you or anything you give me."

In every one of the over 400 eating disorders cases we have seen to date, the individual has *first* developed anorexic symptoms: She says no to food. This caricature of normal development is an attempted statement of *separation* ("I don't need you or anything you provide; this is where you end and I begin—my body and I are not an extension of you.") and of *individuation* ("I am not you and I can control *one* thing in the world: what comes into my body.").

As these attempts at separation-individuation inevitably fail, some individuals proceed from a passive to an active effort by bingeing and purging. Here both sides of the developmental dilemma are expressed. Bingeing or addictive overeating are attempts to create a need-satisfying person or function (for example, self-soothing). The addictive eating is an effort to fill the emptiness of depression and the absence of self-regulation. There is a yearning for nurturing, characterized by consuming a "good" object (food), and expelling a "bad object" (acidic vomitus). The bulimic individual expresses her intense anger at those who fail to meet her needs by denying need. Her effort at self-regulation in a cycle of bingeing and purging metaphorically states that "I will take you in my own way and I will vomit you out and be without you, proving that I don't need you." She attempts to incorporate what is good, soothing, nurturing, and essential to life, to be independent of the need for others, and to anesthetize painful affects with food.

The bingeing briefly provides the illusion that all the emotional hunger of the past is being satisfied, as if a dream comes true. The "magic" of early childhood is incorporated in the binge and purge: hurts, rebuffs, and feelings of emptiness are soothed, and all sense of responsibility and consequences are subsequently expelled. This reenacts the nonseparation and nonindividuation of early childhood. The process is designed to avoid mourning the past and to extract a feeling of nurturance. But in the end, a symbol is only a symbol. Food is at best a disappointing counterfeit for a genuine emotional life.

Eating-disordered patients come to be aware that their interactions with food are representations of other interactions and feelings. Here is how two bulimics characterize their binges:

> I get really intensely angry—then I'll binge. When I vomit, it's as if all the food is like all the feelings I've pushed back and am afraid of— then when I get rid of what I'm full of—it's like I get rid of everything I don't want—vomit them right out. It works.

> Bingeing is a dream come true—there is one area in my whole life where I can have anything and everything I want. All my fantasies of having no limits or bounds are here, and I don't even have to experience the consequences of getting fat.

A binge actually supplies what is missing—it is the restitutive effort that creates a momentary illusion of having anything and everything that the bulimic wants. The anorexic uses food as a vehicle in the process of deprivation and opposition; she denies that her body needs food to oppose her awareness of needing others and to demonstrate that she is without needs of any sort, even for physical nurturance.

There are many impulsive, addictive, or unrelenting behaviors that are designed to evoke or establish a boundary or selfobject regulatory function. A binge may be intended to fill a sense of emptiness and despair or to anesthetize the individual from the painful awareness that she is connected neither to another nor to herself.

Vignette 2: Bulimia Nervosa as an Attempted Restitution of a Ruptured Selfobject Bond

The patient became bulimic when she was age 13. At that time, her parents began having serious difficulties with their marriage. With a withdrawal of her parents into their own problems and needs, a thinly veiled abandonment depression was crystallized in this already-depleted young girl. She was on the brink of becoming symptomatic with the mounting tensions of pubescence, the associated bodily changes, and the increased social pressure at school, and her parents' emotional estrangement was the additional stressor that could not be tolerated.

She began to compensate for the loss of connectedness with her parents by binge eating. She could magically construct her parents in her mind as she ate and be completely in control of a source of nurturance. By displaying her behavior to her parents, she could elicit predictable (although negative) responses from them and force them to engage rather than withdraw from her.

When her parents did not respond immediately and exactly as she wanted—as an extension of her desire and interest—she became enraged. She was thus confronted with her separateness, distinctness, and disconnectedness from them and others.

She would at first refuse food, pushing it back at the table. Her action metaphor said, "I don't need food or anyone else," and, "I'm pushing back the anger I am full of." She later binged, creating feelings of being nurtured and provided for, as if she could have anything and everything she wanted—like childhood restored. The binge focused her pain on her distended stomach, and she came to prefer the discomfort of a stomach engorged with food to the discomfort of a consciousness engorged with rage, or the discomfort of emptiness.

During therapy she became aware that her focus during the binge was always on what she could have *next*, never what she had at the moment. What she could eat next kept the illusion of satisfaction seemingly only a bite away. She reflected, "It's like I'm looking for something, but never finding it. The food isn't it."

By "looking for the answer," she maintained the hope that perfect satisfaction (just the right food) would be only one step away. The food chosen was always "taboo" (sweets), which confirmed her feeling that she was bad for eating in the way she did.

Her purge was a symbolic release of the fullness of anger *and* of her need for anyone or anything external. She would then ask her parents for something she knew would be refused, such as permission to stay out until 1:00 A.M. As planned, they refused, and she became angry, with two results: She had engineered a situation in which she controlled where, when, and how circumstances would unfold, and she had an opportunity to focus her anger at her parents, again becoming the victim—but *predictably* and *by her own hand.*

By reviewing this sequence in therapy, assessing the *internal* as well as external scenarios, she came to recognize her own self-abandonment as she experienced the rupture of a self-object bond. The resultant emptiness, which she had attempted to fill with food, could be examined as an active process of her failed self-empathy.

These events, and the onset of her bulimia, appeared at the developmental juncture of the recognition of her parents as entities distinct from her, the objectification of parents as people with problems and human feelings. This traumatic disillusionment complicated her already fragile connectedness with her parents and her sense of self.

Vignette 3: Traumatic Loss and Attempted Restitution via Food

Anne, a 24-year-old nurse, presented with a 14-year history of bulimia nervosa. She had binged and purged to the extent that she had eroded tooth enamel, become amenorrheic, and was performing poorly at work.

As we examined in detail the scenario of a binge, Anne revealed that her favorite binge item was chocolate chip cookies. She would eat two to three bags of these cookies when she came home from work each afternoon, alone at home. In examining the emotional significance of such a specific food item and the history of food in her family, Anne recalled her father giving her chocolate chip cookies when he would return home after being away for some time, and how they would sit and talk of what had occurred during their separation.

Anne then recalled that her bulimic episodes began with a chocolate chip cookie binge at age 10, immediately after her father died.

She had been able to create the illusion of his presence with each binge, with the transient fullness and satisfaction of his presence—precisely at times when her empty house confronted her with his absence and her loneliness.

Both patient and therapist must come to recognize the sense of power experienced during the binge, as well as the disillusionment and disappointment that follow awareness that the restitutive effort is limited in its scope and durability, that it does not create a permanent experience or structural change.

The shift from cognition-verbalization to action-bodily focus itself represents a regression to an earlier point of arrested ego development. The bodily focus of the impulsive act is the supremely concrete approach to regulation of internal experience: attacking the physical source of uncomfortable experiences, affects, and perceptions. The entire sequence of action achieves a bodily experience that serves to establish a certain groundedness in one's body and thus a basis for a reorganization effort.

Therapeutic Overview

Eating-disordered patients share a narcissistic vulnerability based on developmental arrest of body self and psychological self. When aggravated by an interruption in the emotional availability of an important other, the incomplete self enters a cycle of hurt, anger, and disorganization. The individual's response to the experience of a depleted, empty self is typically an attempt to gain control of forces regulating the unpleasant affect. The effort of attempted restitution of the selfobject involves the symbolic equation of food. In bulimia, the individual takes on the symbolic selfobject; in anorexia, she restricts or denies the need for the missing selfobject.

Restitutive and organizing efforts are designed to create or restore a perception of body boundary and integrity, and to establish contact with a lost (empathically disconnected) selfobject. The unconscious fantasy around which this activity is organized is that once contact is made, the person within that fragile body and self-selfobject boundary will be complete.

The maladaptive attempt to compensate for a porous, vague, or ineffective body and ego boundary must be a central issue in therapy. Often, the symptomatic results (i.e., disordered eating behaviors) become the therapeutic focus, and the initiating dynamic is not addressed; any therapeutic change realized in this manner would be quite literally superficial.

The eating-disordered patient's subjective experience is one of typically feeling hopelessly lost, empty, and losing form. The selfobject had been functioning, prior to the narcissistic injury, as a referent and regulator to maintain form and boundary functions. With the withdrawal or unavailability of that selfobject, the individual must precipitously rely only on her own vague or nonformed boundaries and internal regulation. These incomplete and indistinct body boundaries do not provide an adequate vessel for a solid, cohesive, consistent sense of self.

CONCLUSION

Inherent in every new step toward autonomy is the threat of loss. The lifelong mourning process of separation commits us to a continuous search for replacement symbols (20). As differentiation takes place in normal development, the capacity to represent the absent object is internalized and instilled with affect.

Developmentally, an individual becomes aware of his own body sensations first through the mother's mirroring, then from within himself. Later, the individual defines an internal representation of his body as he develops the capacity for mental imagery. Later still, with the capacity for language, abstractions become available for the images and experiences of the body, thoughts, and feelings. The shaping of the self occurs in the orbit of the body as well as of the psyche, and especially in the consistent integration of the two. This normal developmental sequence informs the approach to therapy when development has been abnormal.

A process has been described that includes a precipitant of a narcissistic injury in a person who has a developmental deficit of certain empathic developmental experiences due to the emotional and physical unconnectedness of a parent. The fantasies and actions that are the symptom sequence serve as restitutive efforts (directed at the body as well as at the psyche) to create an illusion of a present, empathic parent(s), and, ultimately, are attempts to fill or create missing psychic structure.

The process of narcissistic vulnerability, disorganization, and restitutive attempts must be examined from both intrapsychic and interpersonal perspectives.

REFERENCES

1. Krueger, D. & Schofield, E. An integration of verbal and non-verbal therapies in disorders of the self: II. Presented at National Coalition of Arts Therapies Association, New York, 1985.
2. Krueger, D. The "parent loss" of empathic failures and the model symbolic restitution of eating disorders. In D. Dietrich, & P. Shabad (Eds.), *The Problem of Loss and Mourning: New Psycho-analytic Perspectives.* New York: International Universities Press, 1988.
3. Bruch, H. *The golden cage.* Boston: Harvard University Press, 1978.
4. Bruch, H. *Eating disorders.* New York: Basic Books, 1973.
5. Sugarman, A., & Karash, C. The body as transitional object in bulimia. *International Journal of Eating Disorders, 1*:57–67, 1982.
6. Krueger, D., & Schofield, E. An integration of verbal and nonverbal therapies in eating disorders patients. *Arts in Psychotherapy, 13*:323–331, 1987.
7. Stroker, M., Goldberg, I., Green, J., & Saxon, J. Body image disturbances in anorexia nervosa during the acute and recuperations period. *Psychological Medicine, 9*:695–901, 1979.

8. Garner, D. & Garfinkel, P. Body image in anorexia nervosa: Measurement, theory and clinical implications. *International Journal of Psychiatry in Medicine, 11:*263–284, 1981.

9. Rizzuto, A., Peterson, M. & Reed, M. The pathological sense of self in anorexia nervosa. *Psychiatric Clinics of North America, 4:*471–487, 1981.

10. Garfinkel, P., Moldofsky, M., & Garner, D. Prognosis in anorexia nervosa as influenced by clinical features, treatment and self-perception. *Canadian Medical Association Journal, 117:*1041–1045, 1977.

11. Masterson, J. Primary anorexia nervosa in the borderline adolescent: an object relations view. In P. Hortocollis (Ed.), *Borderline Disorders.* New York: International Universities Press, 1977.

12. Krueger, D., & Schofield, E. An integration of nonverbal and verbal therapies in eating disorders patients. Bulimia/Anorexia Self-Help Third International Conference, St. Louis, 1984.

13. Krueger, D., & Schofield, E. An integration of verbal and nonverbal therapies in disorders of the self. National American Dance Therapy Association Meeting, Boston, 1984.

14. Winnicott, D. *Playing and reality.* New York: Basic Books, 1971.

15. Segal, H. Notes on symbol formation. *International Journal of Psycho-Analysis, 38:*391–397, 1957.

16. Segal, H. On symbolism. *International Journal of Psycho-Analysis, 59:*315–319, 1978.

17. Mahler, M. *On human symbiosis and the vicissitudes of individuation, Vol. 1, Infantile psychosis.* New York: International Universities Press, 1968.

18. Schwaber, E. A particular perspective on analytic listening. *Psychoanalytic Study of the Child, 38:*519–546, 1983.

19. Krueger, D. *Success and the fear of success in women.* New York: The Free Press, 1984.

20. Rizzuto, A., Peterson, M., & Reed, M. The pathological sense of self in anorexia nervosa. *Psychiatric Clinics of North America, 4:*471–487, 1971.

7

The "Parent Loss" of
Empathic Failures and
Symbolic Restitutions

PARENT LOSS AND DEVELOPMENTAL ARREST

The developmental consequences of parent loss by death or continuous separation in childhood as examined by clinical investigators
has been well described (1–5). The cumulative evidence from these
data is that the meaning, impact, and consequences of parent loss on
emotional development and resultant adulthood psychopathology are
determined by several factors. Chief among these are the phase-
sensitive developmental issues (i.e., when in developmental time the
loss occurred) (4), the unique interpretation by the child of the loss
(the "personal myth" developed, including perception and fantasy of
cause and effect)(1–4), the sex of the child vis-à-vis the sex of the lost
parent (4), and the quality of parenting after loss. Specific issues arise
in the treatment of adults as a derivative of earlier parent loss, and
must be considered as they relate to developmental diagnosis, thera-

peutic alliance, transference, countertransference, mourning, and termination (1, 3).

The initial consideration was of the parent-loss patient, who as a consequence of the loss of a parent, had subsequent difficulty in forming intimate attachments in adult life, difficulty in establishing a therapeutic alliance, and difficulty with particular types of transference phenomenon. Pioneering work in the area of understanding parent loss psychodynamics has been done by Fleming (4) and Pollock (5), and their work reminds us how the loss of a parent may also become a nucleus around which elements of conflict and developmental arrest become organized. The loss *event* is important as well as the loss *process*. The loss process entails the chain of events preceding, set in motion by, and subsequent to the loss. The loss itself may represent and bring into sharp focus earlier deprivation as well.

The actual loss due to death or continuous separation of a parent during development imposes an actual trauma with resultant intrapsychic organization, which frequently provides a sensitizing precursor for any subsequent experience of loss. Certain subsequent experiences of loss in adult life (significant others, health, physical disability) resonate with this sensitivity, predisposing toward depressions and other overdetermined symptoms (6).

These concepts based on trauma and object relationships extend also to the relationship between early parent loss and narcissistic pathology. The actual loss of a parent between the ages of two and four (age two being when there is sufficient self and other differentiation to experience the loss of another as a distinct object) profoundly affects narcissistic development and object relationships (3). Idealization and restitution fantasies involving the lost parent are predominant. These children develop fantasies centering around the theme of an eventual return of the lost parent. Daydreams are embroidered with idealization and fantasies that the real parent is gifted, wealthy, famous, or aristocratic. Being unable to register or comprehend the concept of permanent or absolute loss at this time, the child imposes restitutive fantasies and maintains an idealized image of the parent, who he or she hopes will return. These preoedipal losses become

emotionally organized around narcissistic issues and fear of abandonment.

EMPATHIC FAILURE AS LOSS

It is evident in clinical work that certain *empathic failures* have results
similar to *actual loss* of a parent. These empathic failures—experienced as the loss of emotional connectedness and bonding with a
parent—are experienced as emotional loss just as "real" as an actual
physical loss of a parent by separation or death. The empathic loss
(failure) also involves similar attempts of restitution and reunion.

The previous chapters summarize the empathic matrix and process in which body self and psychological self are formed and integrated. These empathic failures beginning in preoedipal, even
preverbal, time have profound impact on subsequent development.
The most vivid illustrations of the developmental impact of empathic
failure upon both body and psychological self are those symptoms (1)
that involve both the body self and psychological self, and (2) in
which the ruptured selfobject bond is symbolically replaced. Clinical
vignettes will illustrate the attempted restitutions for earliest failed
empathy (self-regulation) to later replacement of a missing object
(loss of a parent as a distinct object).

EMPATHY AND THE NORMAL DEVELOPMENT OF THE SELF:
A SUMMARY

The accurate mirroring by the parents of the sensations and feeling arising from inside the developing infant and toddler form the
core of a body self and awareness that crystallizes into a body image.
This body image is the foundation of the emerging development of a
self image.

The first awareness of the infant is an awareness of (being reflected
in) the mother's eyes, of physical sensations and body presence as
outlined by the mother's hands. Vocalizations and eye-to-eye contact
resonate with the affective state of the infant—and vice versa—so
that the pair are intimately in tune with each other. The mother's mirroring of the infant reinforces, affirms, and forms the baby's sense of

itself. Empathic, consistent, and accurate mirroring encourages the development of a body self cohesiveness from the unorganized sensory experiences of the infant.

For the infant, reality is the infant's body as defined by the mother's response, as she is viewed as an accurate mirror of the infant. The accuracy of mirroring is thus crucial.

The developmental task is the formation of a stable, integrated, cohesive mental representation of one's body—a core body image: what is inside, what is outside, and clear, distinct boundaries between the two. This creation of an individual internal space occurs simultaneously with the evolving psychological self.

Under most ordinary circumstances, there is parallel development of body self and psychological self: the dual awareness of establishing body boundaries and delineating internal body states is coherent and consistent, and is integrated with the parallel development of affective, cognitive, and motoric maturation. In normal development, this unity is a natural synthesis.

EMPATHIC FAILURES: DEVELOPMENTAL DEFICIT AS "PARENT LOSS"

If the sensations, movements, and affects generated by the infant are not met and affirmed to some significant and accurate extent, or if they are supplanted by the mother's own needs and internal state projected onto the baby, the infant must comply. Although these empathic failures may occur in varying forms throughout development, an initial and significant failure of development of a distinct body image results in an inability to recognize an internal focus of sensation as an internal point of reference. The nucleus of this pathological process is in the earliest phase of the formation of the nascent sense of self: in the autistic and symbiotic stages of life—that is, in the first weeks and months of life—*before* separation-individuation begins.

The earliest body image and subsequent self images are the response to the empathic reflections of significant others in the external world. The mental representations that are formed are then affected by the process and nature of interactions, as well as by an interruption of that process. The experience of another individual as a selfobject, most predominant in early development, concurs with the experience of the loss of that selfobject as loss of continuity of both body self and psychological self.

I have described three categories of empathic failure in the establishment of body self resulting in disrupted narcissistic development, and will here summarize their impact and consequence.

1. empathic unavailability (i.e., nonresponse) of parents
2. parental overintrusiveness
3. parental inconsistency or selectivity of response

Empathic Unavailability and Nonresponse

From infancy onward, these mothers have not been able to connect and resonate accurately with internal experiences of the infant. Body boundaries may have not been consistently outlined by caress, touch, or secure holding. As they become older, these individuals experience their body self and image as overly large, disproportionate, misshapen (7). Their projective drawing and mental images of their bodies are *distorted, without shape,* and *excessively large.* They stimulate their skin in various ways to affirm and delineate their body boundary: wearing loose clothes to feel the rubbing and skin stimulation, wrist-cutting, compulsive sexuality. Stimulation of internal body awareness includes bingeing, vomiting, laxatives, or diuretics. Examples include bulimics and borderline personality disorders.

Overly Intrusive Parents

These mothers remain in a mergerlike state with their infant/child/adolescent/adult—disallowing separateness and growth to an autonomous self. The body self and image is experienced by these individuals as easily invaded. The body boundaries in projective drawings are either *indistinct* and *blurred* (8) or *small, prepubescent, asexual,* and *nondifferentiated* (e.g., no facial detail). They experience their bodies as separate from themselves and easily invaded, and guard carefully their body integrity. They may attempt to establish their body and self boundary and distinctness in rudimentary ways: refusing to eat, exercising to feel real, compulsive weight lifting to establish a firmer body outline. Anorexics and other overly dependent characters are examples.

One anorexic stated, "There are times when I *have* to exercise; if I don't, then I would just fade away—blend into everything else around me."

One patient said of his mother, "She fed me whenever she was hungry."

Inconsistency or Selectivity of Response

The response by the mother to only selective stimuli from the infant affirms a *selective* reality. Consider, for example, the parent who ignores emotional stimuli, and responds only to physical needs and physical pain. This model of affirmation is established around the perception and experience of pain and illness. The body image drawings from this group tend to focus or emphasize the center of pain and pathology. Various psychosomatic illness propensities result (9).

Later, the parents may somaticize various feelings, defining in physical terms certain emotional experiences, by saying, "You're just tired" or "You must be hungry."

A failure of accurate, empathic mirroring of the entire presence of the infant, including affective state, body boundaries, and internal body experiences, may lead to the need to tune out or extinguish internal reality, resulting in the lack of internal awareness and the distortion of ego development. Concurrently, the body boundary may not be developmentally distinguished, resulting in the combined failure of both lines of development: a failed development of cohesive recognition and distinction of internal states, along with the failure in development of specific and distinct body boundaries (8, 10).

Parent loss as well as empathic loss in this early developmental (preoedipal) phase can be equally pathogenic. The individual's attempt to restore the selfobject functioning, whatever the nature of the loss, is made through the creation of symbolic restitutions.

SYMBOLIC RESTITUTIONS OF EMPATHIC DISRUPTIONS

Due to the lack of a cohesive internal point of reference, these individuals are more inclined to compensate and focus on something explicit, concrete, and external that can be controlled—an explicit metaphor (with emotional meaning) for what is missing internally. Their attempt is to restore or replace something missing internally by a very precise external symbol. Food becomes a quintessential metaphor to represent the giving, loving, nurturing selfobject who has been lost or has never been present consistently and empathically.

An eating binge actually supplies the symbol of what is missing— the restitutive effort that creates the momentary illusion for the bulimic of having anything and everything that she wants. The anorexic uses food as a vehicle in the process of deprivation, to restrain her awareness of needing others, as if she is completely need-free of anything, even of physical nurturance. By self-imposing a deprivation, she creates an active mastery over an experience that she had previously experienced passively at the hands of others.

There are many such behaviors that are regarded as impulsive, addictive, or compulsively unrelenting, which are designed to evoke or establish a boundary or a selfobject regulatory function. Various "binges" may be used to fill a sense of emptiness and despair, to feel better, to anesthetize oneself from the painful awareness of nonconnectedness with another or with one's self.

Case Vignette: The Compulsive Shopper

Brittany was a compulsive shopper; although that symptom was not the central issue of her troubles or in her therapy, her impulsive, frantic "shopping binges" illustrate significant dynamic issues.

As a child, Brittany had had several sets of parents, due to an early divorce in a very extended family. When she needed money to buy something, she was able intuitively to fit the item needed with the "soft spots" of her various parenting figures: guardians, mother, father, aunt, or grandmother.

Going to extremes in behavior seemed an adaptive way to establish a boundary, to have someone contain her. She would run away from home until someone came to find her and insist that she stop. She recalled feeling depressed all the time and wanting someone to hold her, to wrap her in enveloping boundaries. The desire to be held appeared over and over in letters she wrote but never sent (lest she offend someone and lose them) and in dreams and fantasies. Concurrent with her wishes to be held and her feelings of loneliness, Brittany wanted her own space. But that space never had any definition for her; she either felt smothered and encroached upon or boundaryless and alone. Her body image was as vague and ill-defined as her psychological self.

A freshman in college, Brittany felt depressed and lost. "I've wanted an unconditional love that I never possessed." She described her impulsive use of money as an attempt to possess something tangible, to make herself feel better. She said, "I felt an urge to get something new, to want more, that there's not enough. I never thought I had enough. I never thought I had plenty. I would jump up and run to the mall. I had a powerful urge to go buy clothes."

She described the urge: "An emptiness. I felt frantic and frenzied. An urge to get something more. I'd get very anxious—just like bingeing—the same feelings. Then I'd go buy some clothes. I felt like I couldn't leave without something. Even if I didn't find what I wanted, I had to leave with something."

Spending money as if there were no limit reinforced Brittany's illusion that she could have any and everything she wanted, the same blissful, powerful feeling she described having in the midst of an eating binge. She would feel good—hopeful—as she bought an outfit. The tag became a symbol of the newness, something no one had seen on her before. Maybe she would be different, maybe the new outfit would change her. "I need something there to touch, something that is tangible. I can hear but not fathom the concept of love. I can touch or grab it if it's something." The hopeful feeling would last until she wore the clothes for the first time. As soon as the tags were gone, the feeling was gone.

I indicated to Brittany that I understood that she wanted to give form and substance to her needs. She said, "Yes. That's why I have trouble with and want boundaries. I want to see it and touch it. Whenever I colored in a coloring book as a girl, the first thing I did was outline the boundaries very specifically."

Brittany favored big, bulky clothes that stimulated her skin and made her feel "outlined" and, thus, more real. As she attempted to define her external body boundaries with clothes, she tried to feel real internally by exercising and filling her interior emptiness with food.

When boundaries existed, Brittany ignored them. She would go shopping with her guardian, Maribeth, "We'd buy whatever I wanted. Maribeth would have boundaries, for example, up to $3,000 for me on a trip, but those could be blurred, too. If I really wanted something, I'd beg her and she'd say OK. My father would also give me $500, my mother, $200, my grandmother, $100, and my aunt, $50." The effective limits were never clear. Brittany did not defy the rules; for her, they were just not there.

We came to understand the urge to shop as, in part, an attempted remedy for her unmet need to be held, usually precipitated by a disruption in her connectedness with someone important to her. Clothes were a concrete way of being held and having skin stimulation, just as food was a symbolic nurturing, all representing a valiant effort to regulate her own self-experience and mood. There was a component of family encouragement; her mother would buy Brittany clothes whenever Brittany felt bad. In buying her own clothes, Brittany was doing for herself what her mother would have done to help her feel good. The clothes were a fashionably tailored version of Brittany's old security blanket, magically connecting her with her longed-for mother.

The Family System

Dynamics such as those described with the compulsive shopper must be considered at a systemic level, as reinvolving members of the family who become preoccupied, emotionally absent, or otherwise disengaged. Various efforts, including impulsive acts, often precipitously engage the response of disengaged others (11, 12).

Anecdotally, we have seen several cases in which a girl developed severe anorexia nervosa, in part, as an unconscious attempt to keep her parents together at a time of impending divorce. Some instances have even been conscious efforts. The anorexia provided such a mutual concern and focus for the parents, they became united in an effort to save their daughter.

There has also been an unusually high incidence of at least one parent of anorexic girls who is significantly older than parents of nonanorexic peers—often by a decade or two. There is an equally high incidence of anorexic girls with one parent having a severe physical condition or terminal illness. These situations create in the girl a fear of loss of her parent. These fears of loss by death or separation seem especially great to the girl who is developmentally arrested and unprepared for autonomous functioning. Her illness, then, is a specific attempt to not grow up, to not have her parents get old and die. She may attempt to magically freeze the march of biological time by not beginning pubescence. Or the older adolescent or young adult may attempt to retreat to a "safer" time—before she blossomed into a young woman. The body image drawings of these girls and young women at the time of presentation for treatment show a pre-pubescent, asexual figure—often small and helpless-looking (7, 8).

The daughter's illness also has a specific effect on the family system: rather than being anxious about their own impending separation/aging/loss/death, the parents have an external focus—their sick daughter. Her condition is a specific, delineated external focus, which, contrary to theirs, can seemingly be controlled.

DEVELOPMENTAL AND PSYCHODYNAMIC INTERRELATIONSHIPS

All of these descriptions have a common theme of the narcissistic vulnerability of certain individuals with early developmental arrest that is combined with a precipitant of an interrupted emotional availability of a significant person (13). This change in the availability or relationship of a significant selfobject results in an internal experience of hurt/anger/disorganization and the attempt to control something specific and concrete, which then directly has an effect of regulating both the body self and psychological self experiences via an attempted restitution of the selfobject.

Such actions that involve restitutive and organizing efforts are to restore some perception of body boundary and integrity, as well as to connect with a lost (empathically disconnected) selfobject. This connectedness is to establish a sense of completeness and organization within that restructured but fragile body and self-selfobject boundary.

An individual with a fragile and then disrupted sense of self may attempt reorganization by action. The action has the intent of creating or of reestablishing a disrupted self-selfobject bond. This attempted compensation for a porous, vague, or ineffective body and ego boundary must not be lost as a central issue in therapy. Often the symptomatic results of such an adaptation (e.g., the aspects of bulimia or anorexia) become the center of therapeutic focus rather than the intent and initiating sequence of such action. That is, it is most useful to initially and empathically examine her experience and her attempted adaptation rather than to approach it from the side of the pathological result.

The subjective experience of many of these patients is of feeling hopelessly lost, empty, and of losing form. The selfobject had been functioning, prior to the narcissistic injury, as a referent and regulator to maintain form and boundary functions. With the loss via withdrawal or unavailability of that selfobject, the patient precipitously experiences the loss of form. That is, when the boundary-regulating and internally-regulating function of the selfobject is withdrawn or unavailable, the patient has to rely only on her own vague or unformed boundaries and internal regulation. These vague and indistinct body boundaries do not serve as an adequate vessel for a solid, cohesive, consistent sense of self.

A process has been described that precipitates narcissistic injury in a person who has developmental deficits of certain empathic developmental experiences due to the emotional or physical unconnectedness with a parent. The fantasies and actions of the symptom sequence serve as restitutive efforts (directed at the body as well as the psyche) to create an illusion of a present, empathic parent(s).

The process of narcissistic vulnerability, disorganization, and restitutive attempts must be examined from both intrapsychic and interpersonal perspectives.

Every new step toward autonomy holds the threat of loss. The search for replacements in the lifelong mourning process of separation ties us to the continuous search for symbols (14). As differentiation takes place, what is internalized in normal development is an increasing capacity to represent the absent object: to internalize it, to imbue it with affect, to form and transform it.

REFERENCES

1. Krueger, D. Childhood parent loss: Developmental impact and adult psychopathology. *American Journal of Psychotherapy,* 37:582–592, 1983.
2. Krueger, D. Anxiety as it relates to success phobia: Developmental considerations. Presented at American Psychoanalytic Association Meeting, New York, 1979.
3. Krueger, D. Psychotherapy of adult patients with problems of parental loss in childhood. *Current Concepts in Psychiatry,* 4:2–11, 1978.

4. Fleming, J. Early object deprivation and transference phenomena: The working alliance. *Psychiatric Quarterly, 41*:23–32, 1972.
5. Pollock, G. Mourning and adaptation. *International Journal of Psycho-Analysis, 42*:341–353, 1961.
6. Servoss, A., & Krueger, D. Normal versus pathological grief and mourning: Some precursors. In D. Krueger (Ed.), *Emotional rehabilitation of physical trauma and disability.* New York: Pergamon, 1986.
7. Krueger, D., & Schofield, E. An integration of verbal and nonverbal therapies in disorders of the self: II. Presented at National Coalition of Arts Therapies Association, New York, 1985.
8. Krueger, D., & Schofield, E. An integration of verbal and nonverbal therapies in eating-disordered patients: A model. *Arts in Psychotherapy, 13*:323–331, 1987.
9. Basch, M. Discussion on clinical presentations. Presented at the Eighth Annual Conference on The Psychology of Self, New York, 1985.
10. Lichtenberg, J. The testing of reality from the standpoint of the body self. *Journal of the American Psychoanalytic Association, 26*:357–385, 1978.
11. Boszormenyi-Nagi, I., & Spark, G. *Invisible loyalties.* New York: Harper & Row, 1973. (Reprinted by Brunner/Mazel, New York, 1984.)
12. Lansky, M. Treatment of the narcissistically vulnerable couple. In M. Lansky (Ed.), *Family therapy and major psychopathology.* New York: Grune and Straton, 1981.
13. Mahler, M. A study of the separation-individuation process and its possible application to the borderline phenomena in the psychoanalytic situation. *Psychoanalytic Study of the Child, 26*:403–424, 1971.
14. Rizzuto, A., Peterson, M., & Reed, M. The pathological sense of self in anorexia nervosa. *Psychiatric Clinics of North America, 4*:471–487, 1981.

Section III
Treatment

8

The Vicissitudes of Effectiveness in Self-Development

EFFECTIVENESS IN EARLY DEVELOPMENT

In the earliest interactions between infant and mother during normal development, the infant experiences effectiveness: when the infant smiles and the mother responds with a smile, the infant senses a relationship between the two events and develops a rudimentary experience of his ability to influence his environment. The infant's affective self (1) and body self (2) are first experienced in this empathic mirroring and commingling with the mother (3). Through overt and subtle empathic interactions, the attunement of mother and child promotes the process of differentiation. The infant becomes able to make distinctions in areas of fine and gross motor responses as well as in general and specific interpersonal causality (4).

Reacting to the mother's accurate and consistent empathic responses, the infant develops confidence in his ability to effect events, such as the mother's smile and a broadening range of external responses (5, 6). White has called this the pleasure of competence and effectance (or the displeasure of incompetence) in infant development (5).

The motivation for mastery—the ability to actively determine an outcome—appears to be based in the earliest demonstrations of the infant's experience of effectiveness in eliciting empathic responses (7), and extends in changing form throughout development.

When parents are properly empathic during the developmental process, the child recognizes responses to his affects and actions. The resulting emotional experiences will include frustration, because the parent is not an extension of his body, his needs, or his wishes. Frustration is inevitable; when it is well-controlled and appropriately measured and timed by the parents, it promotes the necessary emergence of frustration tolerance and facilitates symbol formation.

Freud (8) postulated that learning was motivated by fear and anxiety, describing a hierarchy of fear of loss of an important person, fear of loss of the important person's love, and fear of loss of love of the superego (guilt). Infant developmental research and clinical observation consistently reveal that learning is innate and that a desire for mastery of one's body, feelings, and environment is a natural part of growth and development rather than a fear-driven motivation (6, 7).

It is possible for the developing child-parent dyad to fail at differentiation in some areas and demonstrate capability in others. For example, the child may be able to differentiate gross motor responses and interpersonal causality while remaining unable to differentiate the more subtle emotional and empathic levels of response (4). If the mother fails to give accurate or consistent empathic responses, behaving instead mechanically, categorically, or projectively, the child does not experience effectiveness. This failure to experience and appreciate basic causal relationships at the feeling level can exist in addition to or apart from experiencing ineffectiveness in action. If for example, the mother responds most consistently to an expression of physical distress, the anlage of somatic responses and somatization of affect and of interaction will be established. At the earliest level, the infant may utilize gastrointestinal distress rather than motor activity to communicate emotional hunger or frustration (4). Later, the somatization of affect and interaction becomes more characterologically embedded.

A relationship exists between the early experience of ineffectiveness and magical thinking. There is a normal movement from magical causality (meaning that the infant or child does not recognize a causal link between himself and a subsequent occurrence) to a consolidation of simple causal links, to ultimately more complicated differentiation of cause and effect. Practically, this consists of movement from simply crying out and expecting a caretaker to respond, to learning to interpose noises, gestures, and affects, which increase the likelihood of response and need-meeting, to the ultimate communication link of verbalization and symbolization (language) of these needs to a need-meeting person, thereby demystifying the magic of responses (4). This developmental chain of demythification of magic and acquisition of an experiential relationship of cause and effect, which ultimately leads to a cognitive cause-effect linkage, is the essential effectiveness that can be experienced in early development. When this sense of effectiveness is experienced inadequately or inconsistently, the magical implication remains and the differentiation and symbolization process is arrested.

The developing child has to construct notions of causality as he perceives what leads to what. The inference of causality is an effort at mastery, of mastering events by explaining them.

Bibring was the first to postulate depression and other pathologic ego states as consequences of ineffectiveness (9). Opposed to Freud's view that depression resulted from repression of one's anger toward an object, Bibring hypothesized that depression was the collapse of one's self-esteem, the result of the experience of helplessness and powerlessness. Winnicott (10) addressed issues of failed maternal attention at critical phases, especially the failure to establish a transitional relatedness with the infant, and imposition of the mother's own emotional state upon the infant, promoting withdrawal of the infant's true self. Bowlby's delineation of types of pathological attachment advanced the theory of powerlessness and ineffectiveness (11).

More recent studies by the Papouseks (12) and Bower (13) have focused the recognition and confirmation of the innate desire of the infant to feel effective, to want to cause and predict, and to take pleasure in the experience of his competence. Concomitantly, failed influence over events results in displeasure and the perception of incompetence.

DEVELOPMENTAL PSYCHOPATHOLOGY

A clinical model of developmental deficit as being prominent in psychoanalytic psychology, in addition to psychic conflict, has emerged in the last decade and a half, led by the writings of Kohut (14, 15). The failure to develop a cohesive nuclear self results from repeated incidents of ineffectiveness due to defective selfobject experiences in childhood. These selfobject relationships are described as a developmental sequence of merger, mirroring, idealizing, and twinship (14). An infant's failure to internalize adequate selfobject functions leads to the subsequent deficit in sense of self.

Related clinical concepts include alexithymia, the state of not being able to name one's feelings. This nonrecognition of feelings does not allow them to be desomatized, so they remain in somatic expression: psychosomatic disorders, hypochondriasis. Body self and psychological self-development, including desomatization of the affective self, simply have not yet occurred (2). A related, more recent idea is that psychic tension exists in concert with a "contentless mental state" (16). It is gradually being recognized that rather than representing a true repression of feelings, rectifiable by derepression, such primitive states demonstrate the nondevelopment of the internal state into distinct or named or recognizable feelings (2). To experience this state is to feel an overwhelming sense of ineffectiveness and powerlessness, a failure of one's ability for internal regulation and even of the ability to symbolize and fantasize the experience.

All disorders of the self (narcissistic psychopathology) may be said to arise from a basic experience of ineffectiveness that begins as a failure to enlist accurate and empathic responses in early infancy and continues throughout early development. Grotstein (17) goes even further: "All psychopathology constitutes primary or secondary disorders of bonding or attachment and manifests itself as disorders of the self and/or interactional regulation."

From infancy onward, the most consistent affect of a sense of effectiveness and mastery of self and environment is total sensory, bodily pleasure, coupled with a desire to repeat the action that produced the joy of mastery and effectiveness (5, 6). Concomitantly, failed influence over events results in displeasure and the experience of incompetence.

The repetition compulsion is a concept proposed by Freud (18) and sustained presently in psychoanalytic thinking. One repeats past trauma, including feelings of helplessness and victimization, in order to master the experience and alter the outcome. Or, as Freud also elaborated, to repeat a masochistic wish to suffer (19). Through repetition, the past, along with all its unconscious longings and defenses against those longings, is translated into the present.

I would postulate a modification of this theoretical (and thus clinical) position for those individuals with developmental arrest. While the motive for these individuals is to be effective and achieve mastery, they are limited by a past, outdated model. A motivation to repeat past experiences in an effort at mastery is a content focus and assumes trauma or conflict. The repetition compulsion is an attempt at effectiveness using a limiting model of perception: one that was adaptive in a past context, but not a current one. The difference in the concepts elucidated above is subtle but real: that a process (rather than residual content) occurs wherein present perception is organized and molded in a (currently) maladaptive model.

The desire to be effective, to create impact or change, is so strong that its developmental manifestation can become more important than the content or the outcome, as demonstrated by a child's predilection for mischief despite inevitable punishment. The emerging initiative may serve to bring focus and predictability to an otherwise nebulous and uncertain environment, and it may contribute to one's distinctness.

Case Vignette

Michelle, 16, a "best little girl in the world," always tried to please others. Sometimes, though, she would quietly and surely fashion her own rebellion by passively omitting such things as school and eating. When she was questioned by the hospital treatment team about failing to attend a required expressive arts therapy session, she seemed proud of her rebellion and said, "My level warning makes me not like everyone else." (There had been a recent rash of acting out and reprimands on the adolescent unit). "It makes me distinct. It's *my* warning and like no one else's. Nobody else has one exactly like mine. It's something I created *all my own*."

Later in therapy, Michelle was able to relate her sense of individuality to how she experienced her ambitious, perfectionistic family, and to recognize her sense that the only way she could be distinct was to make a mistake.

At times and in some families, eliciting parental response consistently requires being bad, being sick, or making a mistake.

Specific symptoms of pathology of the self represent an attempt to restore a balance to a critically imbalanced psyche. The experience of meaninglessness, dissolution, or a void is countered by a focus on an external event or item, a person, or myth in an attempt to give order and meaning to this chaos. This process is itself a basic attempt at effectiveness. Such organizational efforts range from a primary process attempt to mythify the chaos into persecutory anxiety (20), to an attempt to focus on an external object, such as food, alcohol, or drugs, to regulate a basic affect (21), to more symbolic ordering paradigms, such as castration anxiety or other conceptual schemes. Such symptoms as eating disorders, obsessive-compulsive traits, compulsive activities, and phobias may be viewed as attempts to order imbalanced states.

Alcohol and drugs have inherent properties of their own. Some physical activities, particularly dangerous ones, stimulate the release of adrenalin, noradrenalin, ACTH, endorphins, and enkephalins, which have direct effects on mood and tension.

THE CONTEXT OF EFFECTIVENESS

There are countless examples of effectiveness as a motivating force. Stories abound of workers using ingenuity to control how their jobs are done, of their absolute need to experience the consequences of their actions (22), and of their increasing desire for intrinsic rewards (self-determination and effectiveness) over extrinsic rewards for work (23).

The parents provide a matrix in which the child/adolescent experiences effectiveness and mastery in feeling understood in expanding arenas. The importance of this basic function is demonstrated when there is a disruption in the process. The following case illustrates derailed development based on a type of disruption.

Case Vignette

The patient is a depressed 17-year-old boy, referred for therapy because of a dramatic decline in school performance, from As to all Fs during the year, and impulsive, acting-out behavior. He described, at the outset of therapy, his utter helplessness and frustration with his parents. Both parents are professionals, demanding, and emotionally restrained, who enrolled their son in an Ivy League college two years prior to his high school graduation.

Patient: I think about the past a lot. There is something about being home. I've disappointed my parents.

Therapist: How effective do you feel in getting your parents to respond and to understand what you're experiencing?

Patient: I haven't gotten responses that make me feel good. I can't get their approval. Whatever I do, it's not good enough to really get their approval. It just hurts. There are a few things that I saw as accomplishment, but there is no change in their response. Like my grades; but they didn't say anything until I began to do badly. Unless I really get extreme—like extremely upset—there is no response. When I got failing grades, my mother got hysterical, and my father said we need to talk, and he took off a half day from his practice to take me fishing. It was great.

Therapist: Are there other extreme things you do to get them to respond to you?

Patient: This summer I went out with an Oriental girl. I was really hoping they would voice their opinion. It's hard to recognize what pleases my parents. One night I came in sorta drunk. I don't think they even knew. Both were away at board meetings. Then I regret what I do and end up feeling guilty.

Therapist: I understand how much you've tried to get their response, and how in doing things in an extreme way, you feel guilty and get the opposite of what *you* really want.

Patient: I can understand now too, how much I've tried. And also how it doesn't work, and how frustrated I am.

His imminent graduation and need for autonomy focused awareness on his unmet developmental needs and the insufficiency of his own self-regulation. We continued to talk about his efforts, at the intent versus the result, and how the results were that it did not work to either fit himself into or oppose someone else's position, both being external points of reference. I empathized with his frustration and pointed out his abandonment of his internal standards in the process.

During the fifth month in our twice-weekly therapy, I indicated that I would be away the following session, which is particularly short notice and outside my usual tradition of ample time notification.

Patient: You are probably doing a presentation or something very important. (Pause) I feel very shut down.

Therapist: What else are you experiencing?

Patient: I feel kind of bad, empty, not worth much. (He elaborated on feeling worthless.)

Therapist: It's as if you feel worth *less* because of our interruption— that I'll be somewhere else other than meeting with you.

Patient: That's right, and I feel empty.

Therapist: Empty can feel pretty bad.

Patient: It sure can. I feel that way a lot, though. Now I especially do.

Therapist: So it is your experience of me not being here as meaning that you are not worth much. It is your experience of not being effective in getting me to respond as you want that creates your empty, bad feeling. Your experience, then, is *created by you.*

Patient: I never thought about it that way. (Pause) It's not your being away, but what I make it out to be in terms of myself and how I felt about myself that makes me feel bad.

He associated to experiences with his parents that centered on feelings of isolation and neglect. We examined his feelings of worthlessness, depletion, and inadequacy following episodes with his parents of no response or inadequate mirroring of feelings, goals, or experiences. He was able, ultimately, to see that his parents were caught up in their own needs, struggles, and concerns, and that they were not an accurate mirror of him, even though he had considered them to be.

Later in his therapy, he was able, during a period of my vacation, to go into his room by himself, to tolerate anxiety and emptiness due to our interruption without immediately dissipating it in some action. He indicated that he was able to think of me and talk with me and, through this partial internalization, experienced some calming. The evolution of this self-soothing capacity via internalization of my selfobject functioning continued throughout his treatment.

The point of reference for his effectiveness changed, from feeling good and effective only if he could determine how parents or therapist responded to an internal point of reference in self-regulation and determination.

In summary, the motivation for being effective at its most basic level, having an impact on someone else, is more powerful than the content or result of that impact, as evidenced by the negative outcome when extreme action is perceived as necessary to elicit response. In clinical work with these individuals, it is essential to acknowledge their *intent* (the desire for effectiveness and mastery), and then, together, to expand the focus to the destructive *result*. An initial interpretation or focus on the destructive result is often viewed by the patient as critical, and is alienating.

WHEN FAILING IS EFFECTIVENESS

Failure and the Narcissistic Personality

In his ever-spiraling perfectionistic strivings, the narcissistic individual has no end point, no internal standard of what is "good enough." It is not the desire to do things perfectly, in itself unattainable, that frustrates the narcissistic individual, but the endless pursuit, the lack of a standard with an identifiable, attainable end point.

For such a person, failure is a relief, ending the relentless pursuit of perfection. Within the framework of assuming that things will go bad sooner or later, failure ends the suspense; "later" is now, and the pressure to succeed and be perfect is temporarily relieved.

There is, additionally, a sort of mastery in accomplishing the inevitable negative result. In a system of negative expectations, the only mastery that can be achieved is where, when, and how the failure occurs. The individual is then able to start over again, this time from the bottom.

When someone reaches a goal, he must mourn the fantasy that a current goal will undo or remodel the past. Stopping short of a goal may protect a narcissistic individual from this confrontation of grief and serve to preserve the fantasy. A mechanism for keeping hope alive is stopping short of attaining a goal so that there need be no confrontation of the illusion that the goal will provide all the hoped-for solutions.

Case Vignette

Spencer, a 38-year-old executive, presented with a profound depression. He had left three major corporate positions just before or just after attaining a significant promotion, the last being the position of a chief executive officer. What he avoided in each instance was being confronted with the fact that his final success would not answer the questions of his own emptiness and need. He wanted to keep hope alive, to feel that he had within his grasp the ability to meet these needs, the hope that he was only one step away, that he could be effective in filling his emptiness in his own way and by himself. With the attainment of his last position, however, rather than stopping short, he took the position and then recognized that all the "things" he had accumulated were not the answer to what was missing. The constantly renewable, yet unattainable, hope was no longer present. He sought therapy.

Spencer was very critical of his colleagues and underlings. Hardly anyone lived up to his standards, with the occasional exception of some idealized person who seemed to possess near-omnipotent qualities. These were usually people very distant in his life or unknown entirely, such as prominent national figures. His criticism of others belied his own unremitting self-criticism. He had little tolerance for anything less than perfection, especially in himself.

Three times in his 18-year career, he had been at the point of movement up the corporate hierarchy to a pinnacle within a division or company. He became frightened at these times, fearing inadequacy and feeling that "something bad was about to happen" and inevitably bringing it about himself by quitting. Each time was rationalized as needing a greater challenge, "doing all that had to be done," and wanting new horizons. Privately, he feared that once he got to a position where he was not subordinate to anyone else his inability would become manifest.

He indicated how much he needed structure, rules, and standards to guide him and provide a model. In the absence of external structure and a boss to report to, he felt curiously lost. He wanted to avoid exposing himself completely unless he was absolutely certain of the results; he wanted to do things perfectly from the beginning.

Spencer never felt satisfied. He never experienced his success as a joyful achievement but as a relief, allowing him to begin searching for the next move to make to prove his worth.

SOME THERAPEUTIC IMPLICATIONS

Ultimate effectiveness is the realization of one's own goals and ideals, resulting in self-esteem. This process is the essence of internal regulation from an internal point of reference. Whether we are true to our innermost design supposes that we have an innermost design: ideals, goals, a sense of self. Symptoms and symptomatic behavior may be viewed as attempts to effectively restore to the threatened self a feeling of completeness and vitality.

The therapist, in this therapeutic model, serves as a consistent and empathic selfobject, maintaining an accurate understanding so that the patient is able to resume a developmental process (24). Both patient and therapist immerse themselves in an empathic union in order to understand the patient's internal world and recognize his capacity to create presently whatever he thinks, feels, imagines, and does.

Experiments and observational studies now demonstrate a motivation for mastery—to actively and effectively determine an outcome. The quest for effectiveness is not simply one for mastery over external environment, but for the determination, even in infancy, of internal affective states (25). The desire for effectiveness and, broadly, for competence, is a demonstrable factor in psychic development as early as four months of age. An infant's basic goal is to function competently, to be a cause; the establishment of contingent control over external and internal events is the infant's reward.

Psychoanalysis and psychoanalytic therapy have neglected the developmental course of the basic motivation for competence and pleasure in being a cause. The normal, as well as the pathological, development of this basic motivation for mastery of one's own body, emotions, and environment deserves particular attention, especially in disorders of the self. Throughout our lives, we want to learn, perform, master, and experience pleasure at mastery. The desire for effectiveness and a sense of control changes in form and content throughout development, yet the process is ubiquitous.

The entire caregiving system, including parents, continually adapts to facilitate the increasing regulatory capacity of the developing child. The system, whether family or therapy, must acknowledge the individual as his own agent and facilitate an expansion of internal regulatory capacities. The experience of effectiveness is central. The caregiver facilitates goal realization and provides conditions conducive to the child's initiation of goal-organized behavior throughout the development spectrum. These behaviors become more complex and sophisticated during the process of development, and the caregiving system must allow, as well as promote, the broadening of the child's organizing capacity and ever-expanding scope of effectiveness.

The basis of cure in psychotherapy and psychoanalysis is an enhancement of self-mastery: the resolution of internal conflict combined with the individual's growth to form and perform functions previously fulfilled in the self-selfobject context. This process, called transmuting internalization by Kohut (14), includes creation of an internal representation of the body/psychological self, with an internal cohesive structure as the center of regulation and initiative.

REFERENCES

1. Emde, R. The prerepresentational self. *Psychoanalytic Study of the Child, 38:*165–192, 1983.
2. Lichtenberg, J. The testing of reality from the standpoint of the body self. *Journal of the American Psychoanalytic Association, 26:*357–385, 1978.
3. Winnicott, D. *Playing and reality.* New York: Basic Books, 1971.
4. Greenspan, S. *Psychopathology and adaptations in infancy and earliest childhood.* New York: International Universities Press, 1981.
5. White, R. Motivation reconsidered: The concept of competence. *Psychological Review, 66:*297–333, 1959.
6. Beebe, A., & Demos, V. Affect and the development of the self: A new frontier. Presented at Annual Self Psychology Conference, New York, 1985.
7. Lichtenberg, J. *Psychoanalysis and infant research.* Hillsdale, NJ: The Analytic Press, 1985.
8. Freud, S. *The Ego and the Id (Standard ed., Vol. 19, pp. 12–60). London: The Hogarth Press, 1923.

9. Bibring, E. The mechanism of depression. In P. Greenacre (Ed.), *Affective disorders* (pp. 13–48). New York: International Universities Press, 1953.

10. Winnicott, D. *The maturational process and the vacilitating environment.* New York: International Universities Press, 1965.

11. Bowlby, J. *Attachment and loss* (Vol. 1 [1969]; Vol. 2 [1973]; Vol. 3 [1980]). New York: Basic Books.

12. Papousek, H., & Papousek, M. Cognitive aspects of preverbal social interaction between human infants and adults. In Chicago Foundation Symposium, *Parent-Infant Interaction.* New York: Associated Scientific Publishers, 1975.

13. Bower, T. *A primer of infant development.* San Francisco: W. H. Freeman, 1977.

14. Kohut, H. *The restoration of the self.* New York: International Universities Press, 1977.

15. Kohut, H. *How psychoanalysis cures.* Hillside, NJ: The Analytic Press, 1985.

16. Gediman, H. Actual neurosis and psychoneurosis. *International Journal of Psycho-Analysis, 65:*195–202, 1984.

17. Grotstein, J. The Psychology of powerlessness: Disorders of self regulation and interactional regulation as a newer paradigm of psychopathology. *Psychoanalytic Inquiry, 6:*93–118, 1986.

18. Freud, S. *Inhibitions, symptoms, and anxiety* (1926). London: The Hogarth Press, 1948.

19. Freud, S. The economic principle in masochism (1924). In *Collected Papers* (Vol. 2, pp. 255–268). London: The Hogarth Press, 1933.

20. Klein, M. The Oedipus complex in the light of early anxiety. In *Contributions to psycho-analysis, 1921–1945* (pp. 339–390). London: The Hogarth Press, 1948.

21. Krueger, D. Loss and restitution in eating disorder patients. In D. Dietrich, & P. Shabad (Eds.), *The problem of loss and mourning: New psychoanalytic perspectives.* New York: International Universities Press, 1988.

22. Jahoda, M. Notes on work. In R. Lowenstein, M. Shen, & A. Solnit (Eds.), *Psychoanalysis: A general psychology.* New York: International Universities Press, 1966.

23. Glenn, N., & Weaver, C. Enjoyment of work by full-time workers in the United States. *The Public Opinion Quarterly,* Winter 1982.

24. Krueger, D. *Success and the fear of success in women.* New York: The Free Press, 1984.

25. Demos, V. Affect and the development of the self: a new frontier. Self Psychology Conference, New York, 1985.

9

Self Disorders:
A Dynamic Paradigm of
Psychopathology and
Psychotherapy

THE PSYCHODYNAMIC SCENARIO OF
NARCISSISTIC SYMPTOMATOLOGY

The narcissistic individual characteristically suffers from a sense of emptiness, lack of initiative, diffuse sensitivity, and vulnerability to other people. Intense ambition and grandiose fantasies, often repressed, are complicated by feelings of inferiority and an overdependence on the admiration and acclaim of others (1). The pervasive problem is a defect in the internal structures that regulate self-esteem and self-cohesiveness.

The original empathic unity of self and other, which normally matures, remains unmet and is actively sought by the narcissistic individual. The phase-appropriate mirroring and idealizing process is arrested, resulting in a continued quest for understanding, empathy, and integration. Disruption in the tenuous bond to an important other person (selfobject) is typically followed by emptiness and anxiety, which disrupt an equally tenuous sense of self.

For the narcissistically vulnerable individual, it is not the unconscious fear of the emergence of taboo erotic love or forbidden wishes that create anxiety, but the fear of reexperiencing the disappointment and emptiness of earlier empathic failures (2). To try again in any relationship, inside or outside therapy, to get what one needs but did not receive as a child is both threatening and necessary.

The initial therapeutic focus with this sensitive individual, rather than centering on unconscious conflicts and repressed or disavowed wishes, concentrates instead on becoming attuned to internal experiences, and the external focus that has disallowed developing an internal point of reference. The therapist and patient together recognize the vulnerability to disruption of the important selfobject bonds, as well as vulnerability to narcissistic assault (3). Empathic, collaborative scrutiny centers on reestablishment and maintenance of the internal sense of self and vitality, especially by understanding the nature of the psychodynamic scenarios of narcissistic pathology.

Symptoms and symptomatic behavior represent an effort to restore or substitute an important selfobject bond and a cohesive sense of self. The important therapeutic work focuses on the nature of the selfobject failures, as well as on the narcissistic insults that provoke the disruption and resultant rage, emptiness, or depression. Symptoms revolve around the individual's efforts to restore to the threatened self a feeling of completeness and vitality.

The precipitants to the disruptions, the selfobject ties, and the narcissistic assaults are scrutinized. Therapist and patient together attempt to understand the intent of the symptoms, how they represent an attempted restoration of the cohesion and harmony of the self.

The psychodynamic sequence of narcissistic vulnerability, injury, symptomatic repair, and therapeutic growth is summarized in the following description (see Figure 9.1).

Initial Sequence

The sequence of narcissistic symptomatology begins with a rupture of self-cohesiveness. A perceived narcissistic injury produces

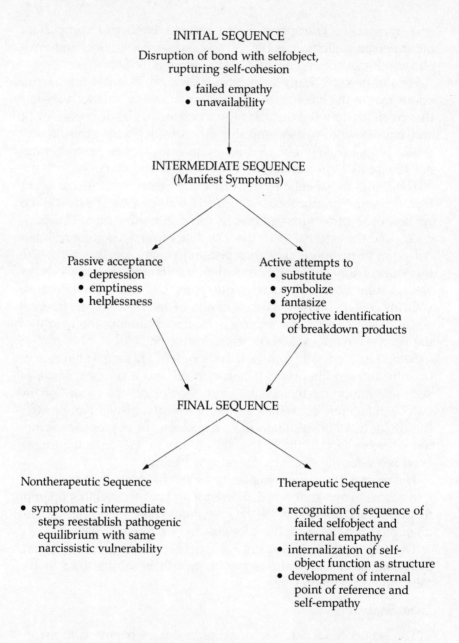

INITIAL SEQUENCE

Disruption of bond with selfobject,
rupturing self-cohesion

- failed empathy
- unavailability

INTERMEDIATE SEQUENCE
(Manifest Symptoms)

Passive acceptance
- depression
- emptiness
- helplessness

Active attempts to
- substitute
- symbolize
- fantasize
- projective identification
  of breakdown products

FINAL SEQUENCE

Nontherapeutic Sequence

- symptomatic intermediate
  steps reestablish pathogenic
  equilibrium with same
  narcissistic vulnerability

Therapeutic Sequence

- recognition of sequence of
  failed selfobject and
  internal empathy
- internalization of selfobject function as structure
- development of internal
  point of reference and
  self-empathy

Figure 9.1. Psychodynamic scenario of narcissistic symptomatology.

fragmentation of the self; the overt symptomatology, often identified as the overt psychopathology, follows as the intermediate sequence.

Disruption in the self-state is provoked by a threat to one's relationship to an important selfobject. This threat may be a failure of empathic connectedness or the unavailability of the selfobject. Recognition of the failure or unavailability crystallizes the wish for a nurturing and ideal selfobject. With the inevitable frustration of this wish, the narcissistic individual feels disappointed, angry, and abandoned. These feelings become the leading edge of the symptom constellation that includes a sense of emptiness, lack of initiative, diffuse sensitivity and vulnerability to others, and at times confusion and lack of focus.

The disruption in self-state and in the connectedness with a selfobject results in overt symptomatology, demonstrating the persistent need for an idealized selfobject who mirrors, appreciates, admires, and individualizes the person. This regulating function does not exist within the narcissistic individual independent of the selfobject; the wish to merge with or be mirrored by an ideal selfobject persists as an active relic of unmet developmental needs.

Narcissistic equilibrium depends on the selfobject to balance the equation. When the equilibrium is disturbed, restitutive efforts are mobilized to share or regain the selfobject's power. The compensatory action may include attempts to exert one's own power and a denial of dependency needs.

Case Vignette

A young woman of 22 suffered from brittle diabetes from age two. Her parents had organized her sense of self around being a diabetic, her diabetic program, promoting a very somatic orientation, fostering the view that every feeling, upset, or sensation was a manifestation of her diabetes to be treated with either insulin or food. Every actuation of experience and feeling was attributed to her blood glucose level.

During intensive inpatient psychiatric treatment, an endocrinologist met with the patient to suggest a revised insulin program and a structured approach different from her past experience. As had the psychiatric treatment team, the endocrinologist elaborated a new reference system, which included the patient listening to her body and to her physical hunger rather than to her calorie scale to determine what and when she ate. This approach challenged her rigid dependence upon calorie chart and insulin dosage schedule.

The patient questioned, based on her old reference system, what the endocrinologist was doing. The endocrinologist reiterated the need for listening to her body and to her feelings rather than guiding herself by an inflexible external program. The patient became enraged, and protested adamantly, "You're not listening to me," when the physician did not respond as she wanted him to: he would not validate her beliefs; she felt hurt, angry, and disorganized, and culminated her emotional chaos by providing a physical focus for it. She ingested large amounts of carbohydrates, provoking a diabetic crisis. This recreated a well-known experience, one she had actively determined. Throughout her life, it had been the only effectiveness she had known; she did not feel effective either in regulating her body conditions in a positive way or in determining her parents' responses to her except by manipulating a now-predictable diabetic crisis.

Intermediate Sequence

The next step is the attempt to substitute, symbolize, or reestablish the disrupted selfobject connection. This step is typically the manifest symptom.

The feeling of helpless ineffectiveness that follows a failure to elicit or maintain the empathic bond must be relieved. The experience of helplessness is rapidly followed by a characteristic affect. Some individuals respond passively to divorce from the selfobject, quietly slipping into depression, despair, and emptiness. By adulthood these patterns have become elements of character structure.

Substitution. Some individuals may attempt to create substitutes for the selfobject's function. This tactic may extend from children who seek surrogate parents when the biological parental relationship is absent or damaged, to adults who replicate original relationships by choosing a marriage partner like one or both parents, or one virtually identical to oneself.

Symbolic restitution. Symbolic restitution may involve the individual's choosing a nurturing symbol of the selfobject. People with eating disorders may use food as a symbol of the nurturing selfobject. The

food is ingested urgently, and then often purged by vomiting, laxative, or enema ("I will accept you in my own way, and dispose of you
in my own way"). The anorexic simply denies or opposes any need,
even the need of her own body for food.

Addiction to alcohol or drugs also typifies the use of a symbol as
substitute for a selfobject bond. While some compulsive-addictive
behavior is characterized by immediate stimulation of the body
(food, drugs, alcohol, exercise, mutilation), other restitutive efforts
engage the body as a bridge to unity; the clearest example is compulsive sexual activity, which is consciously or unconsciously used as
compensation for feelings of emptiness and isolation.

Fantasy restitution. Some individuals may use only fantasy to restore
selfobject function. Symbols and symbolic equations seem to combine action and fantasy, and fantasy is omnipresent with every act,
even solitary action, and includes an imagined audience. The fantasies of individuals with disturbed selfobject relations often resem-
ble underlying mental representations in that they are not as
well-formed and elaborate as those of neurotic individuals. The fantasies, like the relationships, are narcissistic in nature.

Projective identification. Others may actively attempt to repair the
damaged relationship, sometimes using such maladaptive approaches
as provoking angry responses with extreme behavior or demands;
the predictably negative reaction is more valuable than no contact at
all with the selfobject and the associated uncertainty. Various types
of behavior are designed to provoke/evoke responses from others,
usually with a sensitive awareness of exactly what will predictably
trigger reactions from important others.

The period of manifest symptomatology and its underlying meanings, rather than the precipitating interruption in the selfobject relationship, has typically been the focus of traditional dynamic
psychotherapy. Symptoms and their consequences are naturally the
immediate concern of patient and therapist, with the process of
reuniting, symbolizing, or substituting the selfobject occurring later
as an intermediate step in therapy. The sequence involving regression

or fragmentation is most significantly understood as the adaptive restitutive response to the precursor/precipitant.

The perceived and experienced injury to the self must first be understood before the restitutive efforts can be interpreted. The therapeutic relationship with the patient will depend upon an empathic response to the narcissistic injury, and the patient will engage fully in treatment as well as in the examination of a particular narcissistic injury only if he or she senses that empathy. The individual is usually not consciously aware that a disturbance in the selfobject relationship is the source of the presenting symptoms.

In pathological states, the reunion occurs in fantasy or in symbol, and the individual never gets beyond the intermediate state. The fantasy or symbol restores the illusion of the intact selfobject relationship.

Clinical Example

I asked a series of patients with a primary diagnosis of eating disorder and a secondary diagnosis of narcissistic personality disorder to have drawing materials readily available throughout the day so that they could draw their body images immediately on becoming aware of a particular internal state, such as feeling very good or very bad. Their drawings demonstrated a remarkable variation with equally remarkable consistency: when the patients felt bad/empty, their body images were bloated, distorted, and indistinct. Feeling fat and looking in the mirror to see "fatness" usually followed. This was typically the middle of a frequently replicated sequence that began with a disruption of selfobject relationship, emotional disconnectedness, or bonding failure with an important other. The bad, empty feeling followed. The initiating episode was not usually recognized as such, either because it was too painful and acute or because the patient could not consciously organize the series of psychological events and their significance.

What was the bridge between feeling bad and immediately feeling fat? It seemed a desire to be effective, to have focus, to be able to actively regulate internal state. Feeling bad came to be associated with feeling fat, and the feeling of fatness could be effectively attacked by relentless dieting, purging, and exercise.

One patient, when examining this sequence, elaborated on feeling bad: "I want to be effective—to do something about feeling bad. The only sense of achievement I have is feeling that I can exercise and lose weight or at least be in the process of losing weight."

In seeking active mastery, she focused on something concrete which she could effectively control. She might look in the mirror and see herself as fat and convince herself that fatness was the *cause* of her bad feeling. Having inferred cause and effect, she gave form and focus to her dysphoria. She then converted helplessness to action, anticipating reversal of her condition and experience by limiting intake and purging. A transient sense of mastery actually occurred, mobilized both by the causal inference and by the action to regulate the self state.

The therapist might ask the patient what she sees when she looks in the mirror. The usual answer will be, "I see fat." The question then becomes, "When you look at yourself in the mirror, *where* specifically do you look?" Usually the patient will indicate that she focuses on a particular part of her body, such as the inside upper thighs or her stomach; when she sees a slight contour to this part, she concludes that she is "fat all over." This conclusion is based on a particular unfathomable discomfort and the patient now has a focus for her compulsive restitutive efforts.

In this sequence of symptomatology, the desire for mastery is basic and unrelenting and serves as the major motivation for attempts at reparation, coherence, and understanding. The adaptive intent and the quest for effectiveness drive the sequence both in its entirety and in its component parts.

Final Sequence: The Usual Nontherapeutic Scenario

The individual strives for reunion with the selfobject through a sequence of actions, symbolic equation, or fantasy. If the reunion actually occurs, the process of regression may be temporarily interrupted, but growth will not be promoted. Effort expended on repairing the bond or demonstrating independence from the bond cannot be spent on growth and structure building. When the empathic function of the selfobject is compromised, or missing, the internalization of this function is also compromised.

Thus, the usual final sequence is the reestablishment of an inadequately functioning selfobject bond, beyond which the individual cannot develop. Self-image and characterological configurations are crystallized around a consistent scenario of temporary repair but of failed growth.

When the preexisting relationship of self and selfobject is restored, the individual begins again, at least as vulnerable as before, now reliant upon an illusion of the anesthetic and healing powers of fantasy and symbol. The symptomatic act or sequence provides relief initially but is followed by deeper disappointment and disillusionment when it is revealed to be only a symbol of the actual selfobject. The selfobject substitute (e.g., food) is powerful only until it becomes evident that the magic is only an illusion. This is also illustrated in the male homosexual act of ingesting orally or injecting anally a symbolic masculine substance to address the wish to be infused (or fused with) the father's masculinity. The precipitant for this compelling urge is usually a disruption in the sense of self and/or the disruption in a (typically male) relationship.

Clinical Example

A severely borderline young woman developed a concept of herself as hurting and needy, established by emotional neglect and physical abuse during most of her childhood. She reported that the previous evening she had hurt her arm by banging it repeatedly on the door.

As we explored the precise detail leading to the event, she reconstructed the following scenario: During the period prior to her self-abuse, she had established a very open interchange with two friends with whom she was developing a different and open, spontaneous relationship. She indicated that she felt better than she had ever felt in her life. When asked how it felt to feel this good, she said that it made her anxious and expressed surprise at this reaction. She recognized that when she could no longer tolerate her anxiety, she retreated to her room to reinstate the state of pain and deprivation with which she was familiar. As she began to hit her arm on the door, she felt exquisite pain but indicated that this was a relief, that she felt in control by inducing her own pain. She had effectively treated her anxiety by reestablishing a prior state.

The (temporizing) solution to the final sequence can be achieved if there is a reinstatement of the selfobject bond with preexisting qualities. Since this reinstatement is either symbolically or actually consistent with an inadequately functioning selfobject, the same degree of tenuousness and vulnerability exists.

Final Sequence: Therapeutic Scenario

The ultimate resolution to the narcissistic configuration underlying this symptomatic sequence is an internalization of the regulatory functioning by an adequate and accurate selfobject relationship (2). Internalized empathic selfobject experiences promote developmental growth and regulatory structure and foster an internal, rather than an external, point of reference.

Therapeutic resolution includes a mourning of past needs for the selfobject and of parents who, for their own reasons, were unable to provide what was necessary for optimal growth. The patient's empathic understanding may then extend to his or her own experiences and perceptions. The therapeutic empathic immersion requires that both patient and therapist listen from within the patient's experience, including body self and psychological self awareness, distinction, and integration. Self-empathy develops in concert with self-awareness, paralleling self-disclosure.

The therapist serves as a consistent and empathic selfobject within the therapeutic environment, sustaining the understanding necessary for the patient to resume a developmental process. The patient, by being immersed in this empathic union, is encouraged to internalize this self-function until internal structures are formed that take the place of the function previously provided by selfobjects. This maturation process is the central aspect of therapy. It is both unwise and unnecessary to gratify the needs of the patient apart from the need for accurate empathy. Any action on the part of the therapist away from an attunement to the patient will disrupt, temporarily or permanently, this empathic union. Needs other than the need for empathic immersion and understanding are interpreted and related to genetic material (4).

REFERENCES

1. Kohut, H. *The restoration of the self.* New York: International Universities Press, 1977.
2. Basch, M. The selfobject theory of motivation and the history of psychoanalysis. In P. Stepansky, & A. Goldberg (Eds.), *Kohut's Legacy.* Hillsdale, NJ: The Atlantic Press, 1984.

3. Baker, H., & Baker, M. Heinz Kohut's Self Psychology, An Overview. *American Journal of Psychiatry, 144*:1–9, 1987.

4. Miller, J. How Kohut actually worked. In A. Goldberg (Ed.), *Progress in self psychology*. New York: Guilford Press, 1985.

10

Therapeutic Applications in Disorders of the Self

NARCISSISTIC SYMPTOMATOLOGY

There has always been a certain percentage of patients presenting for treatment with vague complaints that lack clear psychological content, for example, empty and guiltless depression, lack of motivation, dissatisfaction, "burnout." These patients come for treatment not necessarily because of symptomatic behavior that interferes with their lives but because of a dissatisfaction with life itself. Their lives seem purposeless, their achievements meaningless; they are lonely and unhappy with their relationships. The range of affect may include euphoria and depression, shame, embarrassment, a kind of exhibitionism, and low self-esteem. There are many typical "somethings" that their "nothingness" has focused on: a perpetual quest for more money, the elusive perfect partner, food, alcohol, drugs. The content and symptomatology of these narcissistic pursuits often receive more attention than the underlying disorder of the self.

These individuals are guided by the responses of others, by external points of reference, so they may not even know or have developed their true selves. A gifted young woman, doing poorly in college, indicated:

> Sometimes I feel really empty. When I feel unfocused and confused, I have no image of myself. I get really scared. It's like looking in the mirror and seeing no image, and I ask myself, Do I exist? Where am I? Who am I? When I binge, I have a miserable, heavy stomach. That's *something*, though. And, for a moment, during the binge, it feels wonderful—as if I can have anything and everything I want.

A characteristic aspect of narcissistic pursuit is the idealization of what is greedily wanted but not available, the perfectly thin body for women, the acquisition of wealth or expensive objects, the avid exploration of new places, or the excitement of new sexual conquests. Acquisition is narcissistically gratifying and provides renewable pleasure, but the narcissistic components of the gratification wear off and are devalued as conquered, producing disappointment, boredom, and the need to escape into new pursuits. The "exciting new" rapidly becomes yet another edition of the "disappointing old." Is that all there is? and What's next? are frequent questions. Guided by their wants rather than their ideals, these individuals see themselves as exceptions, as being so important they can break rules or obtain special privileges.

Such a deficit in self-regulation means that these vulnerable individuals must rely on external sources to supplement deficient internal regulation. Through their reliance on others for affirmation, enhancement, function, and esteem, they attempt to internalize these sources symbolically by acquisition of admiration of material goods and money, or of substances such as food, alcohol, or drugs.

The normal idealization of the future, characteristic of youth, is exaggerated in the narcissistic personality for whom the future may represent exalted gratifications in many areas, such as power, physical attractiveness, wealth, prestige, success, and admiration. When a narcissistic individual realizes that his fantasies are not viable, that aging reduces the possibility of acquiring these ideals, he often suffers an empty depression. Individuals with fragile self-structures react to blows to self-esteem with an array of narcissistic defenses ranging from the search for the fountain of youth through plastic surgery or incessant exercise to the search for beauty in a partner who is an emblem of the desired self. Well-being, however, may collapse with the next common cold.

The failure to develop an autonomous sense of self leads to an excessive focus on the self, as if one's own existence and functioning cannot be taken for granted. Preoccupied with how he is viewed by others and inordinately concerned about making mistakes and failing, the narcissistic person may oscillate between grandiosity and self-reproach in the twinkling of an eye. Such an individual may pursue endeavors to a point, and then lose interest before the moment of actual testing.

Although he may feel as if he is playing a role, the narcissistic individual will often conform to what he thinks others expect of him; there is such a sensitivity to the wishes and moods of others that the narcissistic person does not feel that he exists separately. Words and actions may be split off from feelings; activities frequently stem from the need to be seen and affirmed by others. An eating-disordered patient who immerses herself in exercise to lose weight or improve fitness is often searching for a way to feel real, to experience her body and her self. One patient said, "There are times when I *have* to exercise; if I don't, then I would just fade away—blend into everyone else around me".

Case Vignette

An accomplished professional man was referred to me for psychoanalysis. At our first meeting, he described running out of wall space. He had just received a national award in his field and had placed it in the only space remaining on his walls, which were completely filled with awards and medals. His goal of being in the top 1% of money earners in his field nationally had been met for the past two years. Happiness seemed elusive, though attainable; another award to win or more money to make represented a perpetual series of occasions for hope. He simply upped the ante with each achievement, keeping alive his hope of receiving what he did not get in childhood and of filling his emptiness. (Others keep hope alive by not quite succeeding, not taking the final step across the finish line, so that the symbol is never confronted.) He despaired as he recognized that he was not happy and had never been truly happy and that the *hope* of fulfillment through continued achievement and award could not continue. There were no more senior colleagues to applaud him; there were no higher awards to achieve; he did not need more money. He recognized his orientation to "things" and to the response and admiration of others to regulate his self-esteem. He always desired *more,* but attaining *more* never made him happy. He was finally confronted with his illusion that more would be enough when he had no wall space for more, crystallizing a despairing depression.

In his ever-spiraling strivings for perfection, the narcissistic individual has not developed an ego ideal, an internal standard of what "good enough" is. It is not the desire to do things perfectly, itself unattainable, but the lack of a standard with an attainable end point that frustrates the narcissistic individual and renders his pursuit endless.

MIND-BODY INTEGRATION

These patients typically are limited in their ability to describe themselves and their feelings in a meaningful way. They constrict emotional expression and tend to describe details of symptoms as substitutes for feelings and internal experiences; they inhibit fantasy, limiting their capacity to symbolize and play. Though often quite successful, such patients describe a vague sense of incompleteness or emptiness, a feeling that something is missing. There is often a specific external focus, ranging in presentation from a separation crisis to an eating disorder.

Individuals with more significant psychological developmental arrests usually have an incomplete, noncohesive body self and image. These early deficits in differentiation have impact on the body self, with later difficulties of the desomatization of the body self to its representational position in the psychological self. Lacking a consistent, internally regulated image of a body self or psychological self, they rely on external feedback and referents, such as other people or mirrors. A narcissistic person has little experience of himself as the same person over an extended period of time (1). Patients with profound early developmental arrests involving sense of self do not form a cohesive body image, and there are often significant defects of sensory integration (see chapter 6).

Therapy for patients with early developmental arrests must address the nascent sense of self that emerges from mirroring experiences with the mother in the first weeks of life and extends in changing form throughout development. Distorted mirroring either creates an inner fragmentation which does not allow the development of a cohesive sense of self (2) or prevents the development of a psychological and body self separate from the mother.

Generally, these individuals do not defensively deny body awareness and feelings, painful or otherwise, because they have never distinguished affects and bodily sensations or integrated mind and body enough to split them. The self remains disorganized and primitive. The therapeutic goal is the synthesis of a spectrum of developmental growth, including the earliest stages of psychological birth and growth.

The developing self is shaped in the body as well as the psyche, and the two must be integrated. Therapy with a narcissistic individual aims at restoration and completion and, in some cases, creation for the first time of an accurate body and psychological self. The therapeutic vantage point must include the internal experience of the patient, an empathic perspective focused on emotions, perceptions, causal explanations, self and body experiences, and their evolution over developmental time.

DEVELOPING AN INTERNAL LISTENING PERSPECTIVE

The therapist must place himself or herself inside the entire experience of the patient, empathizing with as much of the patient's feeling, perception, and self-respect as the patient will allow. The therapist must communicate his or her understanding of the patient's experience. Empathy does not mean being kind, sympathetic, consoling, gratifying, or commiserating. Empathy describes a listening position, a particular way of listening from the inside that permits appreciation of another individual's experience from his own frame of reference. Listening from the inside includes an awareness of the patient's internal and perceived external systems and of the representational model he uses to describe his body, psyche, and world, whether auditory, visual, or kinesthetic. Empathy is an observational tool that enables us to grasp the essential human similarities between ourselves and those who are in despair. Empathy, the human echo to a human experience, is a bridge to understanding diverse frames of reference between individuals, among members of a family or group, or among disciplines.

Patients whose basic pathology lies in the formation and synthesis of body self and psychological self have helped us understand the nature of empathy through their particular sensitivity to it. It is by such a failure in the past that their pathology has been created, the sense that their feelings, internal experience, and perceptions have not been listened to.

A developmentally arrested patient sees his therapist as a part or function of himself; the therapist becomes increasingly important as part of the structure of the patient's self-experience. Through dynamic understanding and internalization over time of this entire process, the patient develops self-empathy and self-structure.

In order to establish a therapeutic matrix that allows developmental experience and that becomes an increasingly important part of the structure of the patient's self-experience, the therapist must let himself be used as part of the core of the patient's self. A particular type of listening is required; we must place ourselves inside the patient's self-experience. This mode of listening can be contrasted to a listening position outside the patient's experience, as an observer, a position that presumes two distinct people, the observer and a subject. Narcissistic patients have not yet reached this point in development.

The therapist's response has a major impact on the patient's immediate self-experience. A patient with narcissistic pathology uses the therapist's responses to create an internal point of reference, to distinguish among affective states, and to stabilize his sense of self. Once the therapist understands how the patient perceives him, he need not demand that the patient acknowledge his separate existence. The therapist becomes the personification of the patient's own listening process and a developmental organizer in the growth of the patient.

A brief vignette illustrates this and allows comparison of two different approaches with the same patient. I supervised the group therapist whose group the patient was in and also met individually with the patient.

Dorothy, 33, had been sexually molested by her father between two-and-a-half and eleven years of age. In group therapy, a man (Rick) who had been arrested for statutory rape began talking about the trauma of going to court. Dorothy became openly enraged at him and at the group for expressing sympathy and seeming to condone his activity.

The group therapist facilitated Dorothy's expression of anger, linking it to her long-repressed anger at her father for what she went through. Although Dorothy vented a great deal of anger, she continued to focus on Rick, wanting him to express remorse, guilt, or shame for his act. This therapeutic approach assumes that there is a quantum of anger or hurt from the past that must be expressed, like an abscess, so that healing can occur.

Dorothy's individual therapy focused on recognition of her anger and attunement to each detail leading up to it. That is, we focused on her *immediate experience*, what she thought, felt, imagined at the instant just before she became enraged.

She said, "I wanted Rick to know that I wanted him to apologize for what he'd done. I wanted him to understand me without me having to spell it out. If he really cared about me—or if the therapist did—I wouldn't have to spell it out. He would have said *exactly* what I wanted him to—to mouth my thoughts. If I have to ask, it's not the same."

She wanted this man (as she has other men in her past) to respond as an extension of her, as if this would be restitution for the helplessness and hurt she experienced as a small child. When she felt helpless *at that moment* to get him to speak her thoughts, she *created* an instantaneous helplessness and reparative narcissistic rage.

When we both focused on the current experience, Dorothy was able to examine her assumptions. If I had begun by interpreting her wishes or assumptions, she would have experienced me as critical. I would have been outside her internal system, an observer. We were able to reconstruct her unspoken rage at her mother for not being in tune with her, for not knowing about and preventing her father's molestation without Dorothy's having to say anything. We were then able to discuss more broadly the failed empathic union with each parent, as well as the subsequent emphatic failures which she, via her assumptions, had engineered.

In summary, the subjective listening mode of empathy is the antithesis of projecting *our* intrapsychic reality or theory into another or comparing our realities. As the therapist listens from inside the patient, he limits the imposition of his own preconceived values, perceptions, notions of reality, and countertransferences. The therapist must be able to do this without having his intrinsic sense of self or self-esteem threatened or enhanced by the patient's experience.

Empathy in the Initial Phase of Therapy

Patients may feel embarrassed and frightened at the empathic focus on their internal experience. Archaic needs and wishes, rage, disappointment, and disillusionment may be transferentially activated. The initial transition from an external point of reference, conforming to the needs and wishes of others, to an internal point of reference often provokes anxiety. Not only does this transition entail a temporary separation from the intense connectedness with others, but it also involves turning to an arena (the internal self) that does not fully exist in any differentiated, consistent, and reassuring way.

Greater body self and psychological self awareness require movement away from addictively consoling external referents. For narcissistic individuals, the unconscious avoidance of painful affect is central but should not be confused with defensive denial of painful affect in which feelings are differentiated within psychological structure and actively defended, as in more neurotic individuals. Because of the early developmental level of these needs, combined with the narcissistic patient's lack of internal structure, certain physical actions, for example, eating, exercising, and drinking alcohol, serve to ameliorate the intensity of the need. With a noncohesive or poorly integrated structural defensive system, internal experiences must come into awareness and be expressed via a route different from derepression and interpretive work on defensive structure.

The transition from external to internal attunement constitutes the bulk of the initial phase of treatment. The midphase of treatment involves the activation and elaboration of the selfobject transferences, the development of a sense of self from within this internal point of reference. The end phase of treatment comprises an internalization of the therapist's function as selfobject to allow regulation by a cohesive self, and termination with the false self, including the once-adaptive pathology.

Narcissistic individuals have not come to know themselves because they have been reactive, with their efforts and attention centering around their perceptions of and conformity or opposition to others. When this characteristic emerges in the therapeutic relationship, the patient and therapist can examine it together. It frequently manifests as an explicit desire to do the "right thing" and involves the belief that the sessions are really for the therapist, so that the patient can find out the right thing to do and do it for the therapist. Such individuals are not aware of wanting something independently or at variance with the perceived wishes of an important other. The only way, then, for the patient not to be an extension of his parents (or therapist) is to *not do* what others want. Saying no creates a boundary, effectively declaring, "This is where you end and I begin."

A usual fantasy of narcissistic individuals, sometimes slow to emerge, is of being dependent and taken care of. The patient may enact this unconscious fantasy with the wish or the action of harming himself or of being ill in various ways in order to be taken care of. The wish to be taken care of may manifest by the patient not paying his bill. Dreams and daydreams frequently center around this wish/ theme, which is usually disguised in content. As these developmentally unmet needs become activated in therapy or analysis, the patient is able to reconstruct childhood longings and experiences through recovered fantasies, memories, and current experiences. Missed self-structure-fostering experiences can be revived and constructed. The patient hopes that the other person will know what the patient needs without his having to ask. While the patient ardently wishes for the merger of knowledge and understanding, he simultaneously fears that it will bring loss of boundaries and a loss of oneself into another, a repetition of past processes. The need to be empathically understood and the simultaneous awakening of early developmental needs to be admired, affirmed, and taken care of while maintaining independence may seem paradoxical and confusing to the patient.

Disappointment, disillusionment, and depression occur when others (particularly, the therapist) do not immediately perceive these wishes. Self-inflicted injury, and bingeing, and/or starving fulfill the functions of punishment, restoration of object, and regulation of self experience and mood. The primary aim seems to be a restoration of balance to the self (2).

Idealizations of self and others serve to regulate self-esteem and self-cohesion and do not change readily. Despite the distress that the symptoms and idealizations may cause the individual, they help maintain a narcissistic equilibrium and some self-cohesion and, as such, are particularly valuable to the individual. If symptoms and idealizations are challenged too early in treatment, the patient may flee therapy or feel compelled to defend his symptoms as useful. The initial communication by the therapist of an understanding of the individual's need to have these symptoms and of their adaptive intent is invaluable in establishing empathic connectedness with the patient. Only after the therapist "comes to the patient's side," having developed a shared listening platform, can they look together at the maladaptive, painful result of the symptoms and idealizations and the patient's motivation to get better and grow. An initial therapeutic task is to help the patient focus on himself, to elaborate his experience, to differentiate among internal states, such as distinguishing physical from emotional hunger.

Messages from patients may be complex and require collaborative work to be understood but should first be heard with empathic appreciation in a straightforward way. Miller (3) describes Kohut's way of taking material from a patient in a "straight" manner, as if the material meant what it seemed to mean. This approach allows the therapist to hear material in a positive and adaptive manner, to enter the patient's system, and to engage with the patient in a collaborative exploration of intent and adaptive needs, rather than to decipher symbols to uncover underlying meaning as a step to "seeking and destroying" pathology. It is, simply, an initial positive approach to what the patient says.

A developmentally informed sequence of understanding intrapsychic meaning involves, initially, two steps. The primary meaning relates to self and current self-state, and the secondary elements then may be understood as having interpersonal significance, for example, dyadic and triadic.

Listening for Nonverbal Material

In the beginning, developmentally, there are no words. Words are not necessary to the original self, the body self, or early communication. Before language exists, we communicate facially, posturally, gesturally, affectively, and vocally. Initial communication takes place at a nonverbal, affective level; verbal language is a relatively late acquisition ontogenetically and phylogenetically. Even in the adult, nonverbal communication accompanies every word. In reading written words, we sense as much about the author as about his lexical message. Freud stated, "If his lips are silent, he chatters with his fingertips; betrayal oozes out of him at every pore. And thus the task of making conscious the most hidden recesses of the mind is one which is quite possible to accomplish" (4). Nonverbal information emerges steadily from the patient in therapy. Posture, gesture, body rumblings, voice changes and quality, silence are all meanings of expression available to the apparently immobile patient (4).

Attention to a patient's behavior is not new; however, the understanding and decoding of nonverbal behavior has traditionally been in structural terms, that is, as manifestations of sexual or aggressive drive derivatives or in other object-related terms. Transference material has been understood, until recently, in the model of object-differentiated transferences. What has been omitted in our conceptualizations of this behavior is its preverbal origin. The simplest explanation deserves consideration first: that nonverbal behavior is communication with a significant nonverbal implication. Just as we now consider selfobject transferences to arise from this developmental time frame, we must also be alert to the affective and autonomic communication from a patient.

Nonverbal behaviors are rich in meaning and history and are indicators of motivation, fantasy, and dynamics. Gesture and movement predate speech and reveal basic and powerful affect.

Gestures and movements may be scrutinized for their:

1. Symbolic content
2. Unity of movement, affect, and words

3. Position of the body and interrelationships of the body (position of hands, arms, feet, and legs in relation to the rest of the body)

4. Coordination of verbal and nonverbal movement in regard to timing, intensity, and changeover time

5. Symbolic reenactments: movements that recreate an object or selfobject relationship

6. Associations of the patient to movements and gestures

7. Kinesthetic patterning and meanings in terms of the transference

A recurring feature of the therapeutic situation is the development of transferences that are new editions of the patient's past experiences and responses. Transference represents the continuing influence of a model of perceiving, thinking, and feeling based in the past. The transference process is an organizing effort; the transference content is the resulting distortion. The organizing intent and effort must be preserved at all times in the therapist's awareness. Transference provides information about psychological structure as well as about the patient's perceptions of the therapist; it utilizes the intrapsychic context as well as the interpersonal.

A patient's model for organizing the past, including distant, preverbal experiences, is best understood as an active, adaptive attempt to master the present. The therapist seeks to understand the patient's perceptions from within his subjective frame of reference, neither confirming nor refuting the reality of these perceptions, but exploring their meaning with the patient.

Four basic needs occur in development, each conforming to a specific selfobject transference (5):

1. *Merger:* The mutual sharing of experiences and communication effectively conveying emotional "knowing"

2. *Mirroring:* Forms a healthy pride and expansiveness. If an individual has not received adequate mirroring, he looks to others for validation and affirmation

3. *Idealization:* The admiration of a strong, wise person. Healthy idealization results in enthusiasm and internal ideals

4. *Alter ego (twinship):* Experiences shared, leading to a feeling of familiarity. Without this, a person may feel estranged, detached, empty, and consistently not understood

In a developmentally informed therapy or analysis, these transference phenomena often emerge in this order as treatment unfolds, moving eventually into more traditional object-oriented transference phenomena and conflict-based material. The therapist or analyst must be mindful of this sequence so as to facilitate developmental evolution and help the patient developmentally organize his experiences.

Nonverbal Transference and Countertransference

The manifestations of nonverbal behavior parallel the emergence of transference material; specific body movements correlate with intrapsychic processes. Preverbal and early verbal experiences cannot be remembered directly or analyzed in the transference using a traditional object-oriented model. The therapist's attention is usually directed toward manifest verbal material. Nonverbal material may receive the same selection, reflection, and categorization as verbal material (6).

The first perception is motor reaction. Moses (7) states,

> Primitive perception is closer to motor reaction. The primitive ego imitates what is perceived in order to master intense stimuli. Perceiving and changing one's own body according to what is perceived were originally one and the same thing.

Moses suggests that there is a resonance of the listener's muscular movements with those of the speaker. The therapist who is aware of his own muscle movements and knows which are in direct response to the patient—a sensitive and attuned countertransference—has a valuable source of information. The therapist, essentially, can learn to listen with his or her own body.

Visual imagery that is associated with or that emerges immediately after specific nonverbal behavior may contain important material for reconstruction (6). For example, a nonverbal countertransference reaction (attunement) by the therapist occurs as he unconsciously mirrors a patient who is in a depressed slouch with decreased verbalization.

Diagnostic of developmental need at the nonverbal level is the patient's mirroring and imitation of the therapist as he attempts to borrow some of the therapist's power. The most primitive and extreme mirroring takes place in the regressed schizophrenic who repeats the therapist's exact words (echolalia) and imitates the posture and movements of the therapist (echopraxia). Clothing, gestures, mannerisms, or interests similar to the therapist are other mirroring attempts by the patient.

Vocalization is the medium, the technical instrument by which psychoanalysts and most psychotherapists carry out their work (8). Described as a curative factor in psychotherapy and analysis (9), the voice is an expressive instrument, a conveyor of emotion and a reflector of inner state. It is the vehicle of contact and relatedness that takes the place developmentally of physical contact with the mother (10). Sound and speech parallel physical contact between mother and infant and become not only the first empathic experience with the mother, together with her face and eyes, but also represent the first step beyond physical contact. Contact with the mother is maintained through speech when actual physical separation occurs, early in separation-individuation.

This psychobiological bridge is the anlage to verbal intimacy in the psychotherapeutic context. All forms of psychoanalysis and most forms of psychotherapy involve two people, talking.

Therapists know that patients can, from the quality of the therapist's voice (10) and other nonverbal cues, divine the therapist's inner state. The voice can divulge affective changes, areas of conflict, and a shift of internal states. To a skilled listener, general personality and mood fluctuations can be discerned through voice changes (9). A patient's progression or regression may be indicated by alterations in vocal quality.

The voice and breathing patterns of therapist and patient (just as for mother and infant) may become attuned, representing a sensitive component of transference and countertransference (11). The following is from a patient in analysis:

> Your voice is the connectedness I have to you. It really gives me the freedom to be connected to you, yet not to be restrained or distracted. If I were sitting up—face to face—I'd be tuning in to you and what you are experiencing and what I read from you.

Therapists unconsciously use their voices to calm anxious patients, to soothe temporary fragmentation, to affirm a mood, to stimulate those who are feeling depressed or hopeless. For a patient whose developmental arrest is at an early narcissistic level, the words used are significantly less important than vocal quality and degree of empathy with the patient's affective state. Silence, used judiciously, creates space between patient and therapist and can foster separation by encouraging a patient to explore his own inner space without the intrusion of the therapist.

Empathy and the Activation of Oneness Fantasies

Empathy refers to the reception of human meaning that occurs at many levels and is complexly interconnected. Empathic *response*, as used here, is the verbalized acknowledgment of understanding of the patient's particular perception, experience, and conclusion. The absence of sufficient symbiotic experience during the early phases of development is addressed indirectly in therapy. Accurate empathic response in verbal, analytically oriented therapy results in the activation of oneness fantasies (12).

The evocation of latent, reparative oneness fantasies occurs in the verbal context during which the therapist conveys to the patient that he or she understands the patient's communication within the frame of the patient's own experience. To articulate an empathic response, the therapist needs neither to become involved in the patient's subjective world nor to confirm the patient's view of his world. The significant aspect of the patient's relationship with the therapist is selfobject transference that represents a revival of childhood deficiency states that resulted from empathic failures in parenting. A selfobject transference involves the patient's experiencing the therapist as an important function (merger, idealizing, mirroring, twinship, alterego) in order to construct a cohesive self.

The wish for oneness represents a desire for experiential sameness with a parent or therapist. A patient described by Schwaber (13) stated,

> It would have been so nice growing up if Mother had said, "Yes, I had the same experience; I know about that." (To the analyst:) When I ask you what you've read, what you've seen, it is really "Do you experience the same bodily feelings as I do?"

Under normal conditions and average constitutional endowment, an individual will naturally progress toward integration and maturity of the capacity for abstract thought, an intact self and body image, and emotional development. Developmental arrest tends to affect all components to some extent, just as regression involves parallel regression of body image, emotional state, and thought process (to a less abstract, more concrete level), especially regarding body self and psychological self (15). That is, a patient may exhibit archaic forms of symbolic and metaphorical thinking identical with the dynamics of the body image regression (5).

Peto (5) discusses several analytic patients whose deep regression in transference resulted in their perception of being fused with the analyst into an amorphous mass of indefinable character, indistinguishable from the environment. He describes the development of this phenomenon from different forms and fantasies of patients, some with sexual intercourse resulting in an amorphous confluence; others with some body part being attached to the analyst resulting in inundation or engulfment; another with changing consistency and thickening of the skin gradually filling the space between patient and analyst until they became one mass of indistinct character. These are fantasies of oneness, occurring with a mixture of bliss and anxiety. Peto describes these transference regressions as developing parallel and concurrent with archaic thinking and the abandonment of symbolic thought, regression of body image, and emotional regression.

Silverman and Weinberger (12) present experimental evidence for the thesis that powerful and conscious urges for a state of symbiotic oneness with "the good mother of early childhood" are mobilized in treatment and are associated with positive treatment outcome if a strong sense of self is preserved. They propose that when these oneness, or symbiotic, fantasies are activated via empathic attunement, adaptive functioning is enhanced.

Rose (16) concurs with the developmental significance of the oneness experience, stating, "to merge in order to re-emerge may be part of the fundamental process of psychological growth."

Case Vignettes

Patients often describe imagining what they want someone else to say or do, their own version of a oneness fantasy. When someone's response does not conform to the patient's expectation, he is hurt by this confrontation of separateness. The realization that the other person is not an extension of himself, is separate from him, is painful for the patient and evokes feelings of helplessness. The patient's underlying assumption is that he must completely control the other person in order to maintain oneness and a sense of power. Anger often counters the sense of helplessness.

(1)

A borderline patient in his late thirties became enraged with me during his intensive therapy whenever I moved my foot. He was able to say that his rage came from my moving my foot without his telling me I could do so. He experienced our bodies as one fused entity, and my independent movement became a confrontation of our separateness and, in his experience, a reminder of his helplessness to control me/us. Rather than viewing this as a pathological manifestation, I acknowledged his experiences as evidence not only of his necessary and important sense of connectedness to me, but also as a way of helping the both of us understand more about how that bond with another was an experience missing from his earlier life. In addition, the increased attention we could now give to his feelings and perceptions could be focused internally so that he might be able to distinguish basic bodily and emotional feelings. Eventually, he would know and experience, with a more intact core self, where he left off and where I began.

(2)

The following are quotes from a 30-year-old man in a middle phase of analysis. His lonely, joyless life is largely a result of his avoidant behavior and internal isolation of feeling.

I couldn't merge with everybody else or I'd be lost; I'd be nothing. I had to have and be something distinct—something better. I didn't want to feel so insignificant, like I'd be squashed, or used, or nothing. Isolating myself kept me from having to interact at all with most people. It's a role I painted for myself that didn't allow me to get invited or involved in other things. I was afraid to go (like to parties or on dates) and it didn't fit with the role I painted. Everybody else thought going to the prom was so important but in my role it wasn't important at all; it was *opposite* what everyone else thought was important. And that was important to me. I knew I wasn't going because I was afraid of asking everyone out. I was scared to ask anyone.

I commented that even though he might have yearned to be with someone, it must have felt scary, as if he might lose some of himself.

Yes. I didn't want to be in a group. I would never measure up to anyone else. So I remained outside the group, feeling superior to the group and to any-one who went along with what everyone else did. I felt a strange kind of power, even omnipotence, in not going along with everyone else, and being able to say no and decide myself.

These fears and wishes became activated in analysis as the patient entered a phase of analysis in which his wishes for oneness and his concomitant loneliness were predominant.

Patients with vague self and body images concurrently wish for and fear intimacy (fusion with another). There is a continuing search, either real or in fantasy, for emotional twinship. When close-ness becomes a possibility for such an individual, he is frightened and retreats to preserve his sense of intactness; as emptiness and loneliness propel him to seek closeness, he retreats when it nears, fearing dissolution of self. The relationships of a narcissistic individ-ual are characterized by advances and retreats, rather than by being.

In the therapeutic situation, it is helpful to look at the precipitants of these movements away from and toward and to understand their dynamic significance, as well as at the fantasies that underlie and motivate. The therapist can pay particular attention to the patient's bodily sensations and what triggers them as he tries to help the patient link body and emotional experience. Bodily sensations can be viewed as the equivalent of spontaneous emotional responses, requiring therapeutic scrutiny of memories, current fantasies, and perceptions in terms of the here-and-now body experience. Thus, the development of the body self can be reconstructed and integrated with psychological symptomatology that might otherwise seem puzzling and unrelated.

THERAPY AS A DEVELOPMENTAL EXPERIENCE AND THERAPIST AS DEVELOPMENTAL ORGANIZER

Psychotherapy may be conceived as a corrective developmental experience with the therapist as developmental organizer. The therapeutic setting contains symbolic equivalents of the mother-child relationship, consistency, reliability, empathic attunement, specific and defined boundaries, focus on the patient, acceptance of what is otherwise alienating, and a holding environment. These factors are of even greater importance in the treatment of patients with early developmental issues and arrests than for patients with more consistent internal structure (i.e., neurotic patients). The body self as well as psychological self must be integrated in the developmental march of therapy.

The Nature of Symptoms in the Phases of Psychotherapy

As significant changes occur in the initial phase of treatment, symptoms and symptomatic behavior (anxiety, depression, bingeing, etc.) can be pronounced. Often these changes represent major developmental steps and create intense anxiety in a narcissistic individual faced with major increments of autonomy without an intact core of self. Examples include anorexia nervosa in a girl entering young womanhood, with bulimia beginning the final year of school and intensifying around graduation. Symptoms that represent attempts at adaptation are exacerbated as autonomy looms. For example, bingeing is an attempt to move from a position of dependence on others to being able to regulate affect without relying on anyone else; the bulimic patient tries to accomplish this symbolically through the medium of food.

Symptoms and symptomatic behavior during the middle phase of therapy are often the result of anxiety about change and fear of experiencing the new; feeling good is frightening because it is an experience without familiar landmarks.

Case Vignette: The Progressive Internalization of Self Functioning

The following work on the dream of a 36-year-old professional woman in psychoanalysis illustrates developmental progression of the self and the internalization of self-function. This dream occurred in the late middle phase of psychoanalysis, after various changes made by the patient resulted in the development of an intimate relationship with a man.

> *Dream:* I was trying out for a part in a play. I was wanting to read for the part. There was a woman ahead of me who read for the part. I went up to the director. He said I could be runner-up. I said, "I can do a better job and I can prove it." The part that I read for was of a maid, I think, a black person. I read and did a really good job. People were watching and applauded. It was a comedy part. I was really into it. My body and all—my body language showed it. The director said he wanted me to read for a second part. It was an English woman who was supposed to be prim and proper, but who was really loose and relaxed. I did a lot of ad-libbing. Everyone applauded. The director said, "You'll definitely get a role."

As we examined this dream, the patient came to see that the first character, the maid, represented her previous depreciated self (black) and that she had fit the part well. "He said I could be runner-up" was her dream-indication of her previous concept of nonsuccess, of being unhappy, "almost there" but never completely. The second character reflected her developmental evolution to feeling more valued, relaxed, and content. Ultimately the director in the dream, also a component of herself and her own development, recognized that she had become able to direct and determine her own action. She moved, in the course of the dream from fitting into a script written by another to a position of initiative (ad-libbing). Developmentally, this corresponded to the evolution of her childhood role from being a parent to her own parents, trying to please them and, later, to please others, including the analyst, to an autonomous, internally directed position. She recognized also a pun on the word "play" as denoting her ability to play.

The director (initially, the analyst) became internalized so that the patient (by creating the dream) provided her own affirmation. This function in actuality was not yet fully internalized, so the patient provided herself another person, the director, in the dream. The play on words, "You'll definitely get a role," foreshadowed unfolding sexual issues when the patient recalled that "roll" had been a euphemism for sexual activity in her past. Evidence of the patient's internalization of function and autonomous self-structure was reflected in both the direction (initiative; "the director") and the applause (affirmation). The patient recognized that her dream creation reflected her experience of progress and developmental evolution.

Symptoms and symptomatic behavior in the termination phase often focus on the reexperiencing of developmentally missed experience and accompanying defensive structures so that the patient may say good-bye to both. Although it sometimes has an acting-out quality, this farewell in the termination phase allows the patient a different perspective on the missed experience and the symptoms. Symptoms usually recur in termination of treatment as a curtain call for the "characters" (issues) who appeared throughout therapy. The patient recreates the themes and symptomatic patterns that dominated his life prior to therapy and that were transferentially manifested during therapy.

This recreation has a purpose apart from saying good-bye. The patient is now able to experience the *effectiveness* of *creating* the symptoms, of affirming self-mastery by actively creating the very symptoms once experienced passively. The knowledge that he can create the symptoms allows the patient mastery and resolution. The therapist must assist in organizing this recreation, helping the patient understand its purpose and developmental and therapeutic significance. Viewing the symptoms as a reemergence of initial symptomatology or an indication that therapy has not been effective or should be extended disallows the patient's final integration of his new position while he mourns his past experiences.

Internalization of Empathy as Self-Structure

The therapist's empathic listening and attunement to the patient, with the patient's experience in mutual focus, establish a framework within which developmental process unfolds. Activation of oneness fantasies, analogous to the mother-infant bond, has been described. For the narcissistically vulnerable individual, it is not the unconscious fear of forbidden erotic love that creates anxiety but the fear of reexperiencing the disappointment and emptiness of earlier empathic failures (18). To try again in any relationship, inside or outside therapy, to attempt to obtain what one needed but did not receive as a child, is both threatening and compelling.

The interpretative focus with this sensitive individual, rather than emphasizing unconscious conflicts and repressed or disavowed wishes, centers on the establishment of a basic sense of self and an internal point of reference, a gradually deepening trust of the therapist, and movement through developmental stages with an intact core of self. Interpretations focus on restoration and maintenance of the internal sense of self and the vulnerability to disruption of important selfobject bonds from injury by narcissistic assault.

Symptoms and symptomatic behavior, rather than being symbolic gratifications of unresolved conflict, are viewed as efforts at either restoring or substituting an important selfobject bond and cohesive sense of self. The important therapeutic work focuses on the nature of the selfobject disruptions, as well as on the narcissistic insults that provoke the disruption and resultant rage, emptiness, or depression. The precipitants of disruptions in selfobject ties, the perception of narcissistic assault, the attempts at restoration of the threatened self (symptoms), and the development of self-empathy to provide internal completeness and vitality are all empathically scrutinized (19).

The therapist serves as a consistent and empathic selfobject within the therapeutic environment, sustaining understanding that enables the patient to resume a developmental process. The patient, through immersion in this empathic union, can internalize this self-function until internal structures are formed. This maturation process is the central aspect of therapy. It is both unwise and unnecessary for the therapist to gratify needs of the patient other than the need for accurate empathy. Any movement on the part of the therapist away from accurate empathic attunement to the patient will disrupt, temporarily or permanently, the empathic union. Needs that arise, other than the need for empathic immersion and understanding, are interpreted and related to genetic material (17).

The following vignette, which illustrates internalization without enactment, was chosen because of the sharpened analytic focus on the patient's body self and the heightened awareness during this segment of body self and psychological self integration. The patient is the 36-year-old professional woman in analysis whose dream was just presented; the session is the last before the analyst's vacation.

Patient: My hands feel like rocks right now. They can't move.

Analyst: Focus on your hands and arms and let your feelings and fantasies go.

Patient: They're holding incense. That's crazy!

Analyst: Holding and sensing.

Patient: I am binding them down. I feel it. My whole body feels heavy now, like it's bound down.

Analyst: I think you're binding down some feeling.

Patient: (Crying) I really feel upset. I feel small. This couch is small and you and that chair are very big.

Analyst: What would your hands and arms be doing if they weren't bound down?

Patient: They would hug and hold you since you're leaving—to say good-bye, I guess. I want to be sure that you'll come back. And I know you will. It's like maybe you won't be here when I come back for our next session. I feel like I'm standing up now and I'm a mummy—all wrapped up.

Analyst: What does that feel like?

Patient: All wrapped up—like inside a hug. I'll bet you give good hugs.

Analyst: Like a mommy?

Patient: Yeah. Like a fur coat. (Referring to her fantasy of my giving her a fur coat prior to a previous interruption, analyzed as both a concrete gift left behind and a hug)

Analyst: That was just before I left the last time.

Patient: How do you remember?

Analyst: Giving you a fur coat is an important event. What do you
                mean, how do I remember?

Patient: (Laughing) I feel hugged a lot by you without you actu-
                ally hugging me. I think that happens.

Analyst: How?

Patient: How? I imagine it.

Analyst: I guess it doesn't have to be the actual fantasy of an
                embrace, even—but just a part of your experience in
                here—that you're really in tune with yourself.

Patient: Yes—it's a hug without a hug. A hug without an embrace.

Analyst: That I'm not doing it physically says how much you're
                able to create that inside yourself now—that which
                you've wished for for so long.

The purpose of empathic attunement is to help the patient develop
self-empathy and to internalize it. When self-empathy is absent, the
patient must find a way to develop it, a process that involves both discovery and change and entails the mourning of previous empathic
failures.

Nothingness and frustration at not being able to communicate may
represent a memory, not of an event but of an experience; reexperiencing in therapy is a way of remembering. The purpose of the treatment is to understand, to enact, and to view what was not seeable or
concrete before. Past process becomes present content; a memory
becomes present reality.

In most of the patients described through this book, developmental arrest has occurred much earlier than it does in object-differentiated neurosis. The therapist and the patient with an object-
differentiated neurosis may see the therapy as a chess game, an anal-
ogy of Freud's, with moves and countermoves and a focus on interpreting defense and resistance, the patient eluding entrapment until
the king (the pathology) is finally eradicated.

If the therapist operates with a model of object-differentiated neurosis when a patient has an early developmental arrest, the treatment

may be compromised significantly. Such a position on the part of the therapist may indicate failure of empathy and neutrality.

A failure of the therapist's empathy may result from his not recognizing that both sides of a particular struggle are internal for the patient, whose wish to grow, master, and develop is countered by his equally strong fear of change and his determination to oppose his own best efforts at growth. Neutrality fails when the therapist does not remain equidistant and empathic with both sides of the patient's conflict. If the therapist tries to push the patient forward, to get him better and over his symptoms, the patient has successfully deposited (externalized) his impetus and initiative inside the therapist and struggles to win by countering the therapist's desire to get him well. The desire for change and the fear of it must be seen as residing within the patient.

On Reconstruction

A current reconstruction (before an interpretive reconstruction of the past) focuses on intricate details of the experiences, fantasies, and thoughts immediately preceding the frantic feeling that results in compulsive activity. Usually, fantasies are not well-formed, and the experience can be focused on only if impulsive action is not carried out and the compelling internal experience is scrutinized. Often, the patient experiences emptiness and a desire to be soothed or comforted when a selfobject bond is ruptured. Fantasies concerning food, money, sex, or other acquisitions frequently focus on being supported or hugged as a mother would hug an infant. While such fantasies may not provide the key to discovering a repressed experience or wish, they may still be therapeutically effective in giving form to a nameless and vague yearning.

A patient's ability to delay action in order to look at the urge motivating an impulsive act, and try to understand it, contributes significantly to his treatability. Addictive behavior precludes the possibility of understanding and tolerating anxiety. The patient often requires help in structuring an alternate sequence so that he is not overwhelmed by not being able to take his accustomed action. An example is the suggestion that a bulimic patient keep a journal and write her experiences, feelings, and fantasies as an alternative to bingeing. The act of writing at the time an urge to binge occurs can replace the action sequence of bingeing. The urge to binge becomes a signal that an internal experience is begging for understanding, and the writing may offer both understanding and mastery by giving active form to an otherwise unknowable internal experience. Such an individual's sense of worth is often tied to action and performance; interpersonal affirmation, as well as a return to basic bodily experience, is affected by the action.

Additional Therapeutic Modalities

Especially for patients with more significant developmental arrest, the creative and expressive arts therapies offer more direct access to the unconscious and symbolic processes as well as to more basic experiences of the body self. The methodologies of expressive therapies allow direct experience of body self and basic affect without guilt by bypassing later developmental structures, such as superego, to directly access experience (20). In inpatient or day treatment settings, these therapies can provide nonverbal, expressive, and experiential integration of mind and body through movement-dance therapy, biofeedback, neurosensory integration, sensory awareness techniques, psychodrama, and art therapy. These modalities can be utilized in psychodynamically oriented, developmentally informed sequences and be cohesively integrated with a treatment team. The results can be quite powerful, partly because of these therapies' intrinsic relationship with primary process and preverbal and nonverbal developmental issues. Additional techniques address body self and psychological self development for patients with significant arrest through videotape feedback, body image tracing, sequential clay sculpting of body image, mask and marionette making, and projective collages and drawings. Each of these therapeutic techniques can result in heightened self-experience, an effective communication of affect and internal reality, and an objective depiction of the patient's experience in a form that can be validated by both patient and therapist.

It is important that the drawing, movement, sculpting, and so forth, not be analyzed or interpreted by the therapist but by the patient and therapist together, giving meaning to the drawing by using the patient's own experience as a point of reference. The patient's internal experience is then validated.

The emergence of material rooted in the preverbal period is easily obstructed. It is undifferentiated and unstructured, since it existed when there were no mind-body or self-object divisions. The preverbal period encompasses basically the first three years of life. Although some verbalization begins in the second year of life, the major expressive behaviors are motor, mimetic, and gestural. As verbal and cognitive capacity increase, the experience shifts, and the capacity for verbal and encoding mastery heightens. Still, by age two to three, a child does not yet have language or concepts to match the complexities of fantasies, thoughts, and affects.

Communication in therapy such as inpatient therapeutic experiences with therapists using dance movement, sensory awareness exercises, projective drawings, or psychodrama is not "acting out" but is a way of remembering more akin to early experience. At times, the body is both object and subject of perception.

These expressive treatment modalities can be combined with verbal therapy to promote a cohesive and complete developmental sequence. Integrated therapy begun at a basic level of awareness of body self allows resumption of the growth process in a more profound and rapid manner. Additionally, the patient's desperate sense of helplessness and ineffectiveness is immediately addressed by techniques that deal with primitive and preverbal issues and integrate them with higher-level verbal and symbolic functions and experience to provide cohesive development of a sense of self.

IN OVERVIEW

Depth psychology differs from most sciences in which the observer examines and collects data, reports on them, and draws conclusions from them. In depth psychology, the examiner has to merge with the material; he allows himself to become resonant with his patient's experience and understanding in an empathic posture that respects individual boundaries but fosters a sharing and blending. This is not a regression or total union with the patient. Empathy allows the therapist partial or trial identifications and enables him to put himself in the patient's place, to see and feel what the patient is experiencing and how he perceives that experience. Empathy, a prolonged immersion in another's experience, is the essence of depth psychology.

A basic aspect of therapeutic approach for an individual coming from a severely growth-inhibiting environment and having distortions in the perception of emotional and somatic experiences and communications may be to initially focus on the accurate reading and labeling of signals, both somatic and affective. A therapeutic task can be to focus on those particular signals arising from within the patient that he may be omitting, deleting, or distorting. Some of these signals or experiences may be quite threatening, such as the experience of emptiness or of internal disorganization. As this close attunement of both therapist and patient is on the patient's internal experiences, the patient may fear reexperiencing the disappointment and emptiness of earliest empathic failures once again.

The therapist must respond contingently to the production of the patient. A basic sense of causality thereby becomes established. It is the empathic immersion in the internal and external experience of the patient in therapy, and the communication of that understanding, which provides a basis for self-empathy. The patient can then internalize this process and functioning to develop an internal center of initiative with affect and esteem regulation.

Often the earliest experiences in the patient/therapist interaction are to first develop together a point of reference from inside the experience of the patient, and, once inside that experience with some degree of empathy and consistency, to develop a way to identify and then to differentiate among the various feeling and physical experiences. The therapist functions as an auxiliary ego, a selfobject that is inside the experience and functional orbit of the patient, not as an external, separately identifiable transference person or object. As the therapist helps the patient more and more establish a sense of equilibrium, a calming experience can be identified, a wider range of internal feeling and bodily stimuli can be recognized, and, ultimately, the interaction of inner versus outer can be recognized, with a clearer line of demarcation between the two; that is, where an individual ends and the rest of the world begins. Whenever the patient becomes disorganized, as exemplified by empathic failures, the focus becomes the reestablishment of that empathic connectedness. It is this empathic connectedness itself, the experience of being understood, that provides the calming experience. As the patient feels soothed, the breach of empathy can be scrutinized, thus providing, gradually, a regulation via the clear recognition of cause and effect—and ultimately that the cause and effect both reside within the patient's perceptions.

The ubiquitous misreadings of the patient's communications by all those in his life, thus the failure of all contingent responses, can be examined currently to see the role the patient has in engineering empathic failures: the failure to know himself what he is experiencing, or the failure to communicate that experience to someone else outside his experience.

When a therapist becomes empathically immersed in a patient's internal experience, he notices that the patient begins to treat him in a funny way, as if he were actually a part of the patient, a function; something the patient is not able to *do* or *be* for himself. Such selfobject functioning works to regulate self-esteem.

The therapist must always be aware of a developmental flow, a developmental timetable. He must be able to sense where the patient is at any given point in the therapy and serve as organizer for emerging material. The patient may find it impossible to understand a chaotic and scattered time sequence representing the reexperiencing of his earliest development, which may not have followed a predictable course.

Empathy is itself a developmental line beginning in infancy with the mother and ultimately leading to self-empathy. The therapist must enable the patient to make empathy an internalized structure.

Each step in therapy brings changes: the move from dependency to independence, from an external point of reference and initiative to an internal, and an expanding capacity for relationships and experiences. This book has emphasized throughout the need for integration of body and mind, the system of unifying the developmental representation of body self and psychological self.

REFERENCES

1. Geist, R. Therapeutic dilemmas in the treatment of anorexia nervosa: a self-psychological perspective. In S. Emmett (Ed.), *Theory and treatment of anorexia nervosa and bulimia.* New York: Brunner/Mazel, 1985.

2. Shane, M., & Shane, E. Self change and development in the analysis of an adolescent patient: the use of a combined model. Presented at the American Psychoanalytic Association Meeting, Denver, 1985.

3. Miller, J. How Kohut actually worked. In A. Goldberg (Ed.), *Progress in self psychology.* New York: Guilford Press, 1985.

4. Freud, S. *Collected papers, vol. 2* (p. 94). London: Hogarth Press, 1933.

5. Peto, A. Body image and archaic thinking. *International Journal of Psycho-Analysis, 40*:223–231, 1959.

6. Per Orar, A. Reconstruction of preverbal experiences. *Journal of the American Psychoanalytic Association, 31*:33–58, 1983.

7. Moses, P. *The voice of neurosis.* New York: Grune & Stratton, 1954.

8. Silverman, L., Lachman, F., & Milich, R. *The search for oneness.* New York: International Universities Press, 1982.

9. Stone, L. *The psychoanalytic situation.* New York: International Universities Press, 1961.

10. Bady, S. The voice as a curative factor in psychotherapy. *Psychoanalytic Review, 72*:472–490, 1985.

11. Racker, H. *Transference and countertransference.* London: Hogarth Press, 1966.

12. Silverman, L., & Weinberger, J. Mommy and I are one. *American Psychologist, 40*:1296–1308, 1985.

13. Schwaber, E. Construction, reconstruction, and the mode of clinical attunement. In A. Goldberg (Ed.), *The future of psychoanalysis: Essays in honor of Heinz Kohut.* New York: International Universities Press, 1983.

14. Krueger, D. Body self, psychological self, and bulimia: Developmental and clinical considerations. In H. Schwartz (Ed.), *Bulimia: Psychoanalytic treatment and theory.* New York: International Universities Press, 1988.

15. Donatti, D., Thibodeaux, C., Krueger, D., & Strupp, K. Sensory integrations of body image distortion in eating disorder patients. Unpublished paper.

16. Rose, G. Fusion states. In P. Giovacchini (Ed.), *Tactics and techniques in psycho-analytic therapy.* New York: Jason Aronson, 1972.

17. Baker, H., & Baker, M. Heinz Kohut's "Self psychology": An overview. *American Journal of Psychiatry, 144*:1–9, 1987.

18. Basch, M. The selfobject theory of motivation and the history of psychoanalysis. In P. Stepansky & A. Goldberg (Eds.), *Kohut's legacy.* Hillsdale, NJ: The Atlantic Press, 1984.

19. Krueger, D. The "parent loss" of empathic failures and the model symbolic restitution of eating disorders. In D. Dietrich & P. Shabad (Eds.), *The problem of loss and mourning: New psychoanalytic perspectives.* New York: International Universities Press, 1988.

20. Fink, P. In *Looking ahead, planning together: The creative arts in therapies.* Symposium published by Hahnemann University, Philadelphia, Pennsylvania, 1985.

Index

168 BODY SELF & PSYCHOLOGICAL SELF

Bulimia nervosa (continued)
  journal writing in, 161–162
  psychodynamic aspects of, 80
  symbolic restitution in, 104
Button, E., 27

Castration anxiety, 62
Causality, 115
Cognition, developmental deficits of,
  70–73
Compulsive behaviors:
  repetition, 44, 117
  sexual activity, 131
  shopping, 104–106
Conformity, 36
Contexts:
  adaptive, 88–94, 146
  of effectiveness, 118–121
  in pathological separation-
    individuation, 46–50
  of symptoms, 88–94, 146
Control. See Effectiveness
Controlling behavior, of parent, 36
Countertransference, nonverbal, 149–151

Death, of parent, 94, 98–100
Demos, V., 15, 20, 36, 113, 114, 116, 123
Dependency, fantasy of, 145
Deprivation, 53
Depth psychology, 163–164
Development:
  of body image, 26–29
  of body self, 5–16
  of body self and psychological self in
    integrated line, 3–5
  in body self disorders, 35–40
  of bridge between "self" and "other,"
    21–24
  effectiveness in early, 7, 19–21,
    113–115
  empathy and, 100–101
  erotogenic zones in, 29–30
  interrelationship with psychodynamics,
    107–108
  of potential space and transitional
    object, 21–26
Developmental arrest:
  body image pathology and, 83–87
  in eating disorders, 64–65, 73–74,
    76–77
  parent loss and, 98–100

psychodynamics of, 77–83
  in self disorders vs. object-
    differentiated neurosis, 160–161
  therapeutic approach to, 87–95
Developmental deficits:
  of cognition and language, 70–73
  effectiveness and, 116–118
Developmental experience, therapy as,
  155–163
Devenis, L., 45, 49
Donatti, D., 64, 152
Dowling, S., 35, 37
Drawings:
  of body image, 84, 132
  interpretation of, 162–163
Dubovsky, S., 8

Eating disorders. See also Anorexia ner-
    vosa; Bulimia nervosa
  and awareness of body's internal state,
    10
  body image pathology and, 83–87
  and definition of body surface, 10
  developmental arrest in, 64–65, 73–74,
    76–77
  developmental deficits of cognition and
    language in, 72–73
  object-relations model of, 83–87
  psychodynamic aspects of, 77–83
  psychosexual model of, 83
  therapeutic approach to, 87–95
"Effectance pleasure," 19, 113–114, 123
Effectiveness:
  context of, 118–121
  and developmental psychopathology,
    116–118
  in early development, 7, 19–21, 113–
    115
  failing as, 121–123
  feeling fat and, 132–133
  feeling of, in bulimia, 81–82
  therapeutic implications of, 123–124
Ego:
  alter, 149
  body, 3, 42
  and body self, 13–14
Ego nuclei, 9
Emde, R., 7, 14, 113
Emotional language, 70–73
Emotional sensorimotor thinking, 71
Empathic disruptions, symbolic
    restitutions of, 104–107, 130–131